Building Teams, Building People

Expanding the Fifth Resource, Second Edition

Thomas R. Harvey
Bonita Drolet

Rowman & Littlefield Education
Lanham • New York • Toronto • Oxford

This title was originally published by ScarecrowEducation. First Rowman & Littlefield Education edition 2005.

Published in the United States of America
by Rowman & Littlefield Education
A Division of Rowman & Littlefield Publishers, Inc.
A wholly owned subsidiary of The Rowman & Littlefield Publishing Group, Inc.
4501 Forbes Boulevard, Suite 200, Lanham, Maryland 20706
www.rowmaneducation.com

PO Box 317
Oxford
OX2 9RU, UK

British Library Cataloguing in Publication Information Available

Library of Congress Cataloging-in-Publication Data

Harvey, Thomas R.
  Building teams, building people : expanding the fifth resource / Thomas
R. Harvey, Bonita Drolet.—2nd ed.
      p.   cm.
  Includes bibliographical references and index.
  ISBN-13: 978-1-57886-141-5 (pbk. : alk. paper)
  ISBN-10: 1-57886-141-1 (pbk. : alk. paper)
  1. Teams in the workplace. 2. Employee empowerment. 3. Conflict
management. I. Drolet, Bonita. II. Title.
  HD66.H377 2004
  658.4'022—dc22   2004001626

∞™ The paper used in this publication meets the minimum requirements of
American National Standard for Information Sciences—Permanence of Paper for
Printed Library Materials, ANSI/NISO Z39.48-1992.
Manufactured in the United States of America.

To the best partnership
either of us has ever had
or ever will have . . .

Contents

Acknowledgments

We wish to acknowledge a number of people for their contributions to the content and insights in this book. Relative to the material on team-building, we want to thank Skip Mainiero. Relative to conflict, we want to express our appreciation to Brenda Barham and Bill Paulo. Regarding the chapter on empowerment, we want to thank Carole Younger for her research assistance and the staff of Bryant Ranch School for being there and teaching us much about the potency of empowerment. Finally we want to thank the students at the University of La Verne for being the cauldron in which we have tested our ideas over the years. They are and ever remain wonderful friends.

Note to the Reader

We want to highlight the fact that many of the stories in the book are written in the first-person singular. We don't distinguish between "I," Tom, and "I," Bonnie. We leave that to you, the reader.

Thanks for joining us on this journey of understanding building teams and building people.

Tom Harvey
Bonnie Drolet

CHAPTER 1

Premises

An ancient Greek tale tells of a Thracian king who ruled his land with an iron fist and was hated by his people. This king ordered his ministers to build him a magnificent palace. For five years the Thracian people, along with Greek slaves, labored to build the palace, and when it was finished, it was as magnificent as any king could desire. It was made of the sturdiest marble and the strongest Greek stonework. The king established himself in the palace, but on the third day, a violent storm struck the land. The winds blew and the rains pelted the palace. Amid the thunder and lightning, the edifice groaned and swayed until finally it collapsed. The king lay dead under heaps of fallen stone.

All the ministers came to inspect the site and sift through the ruins. Finally, one turned to the Oracle of Volos and asked how the palace could have fallen, since it had been built of the sturdiest stone. The blind oracle appealed to the heavens, then replied, "People, not pieces of marble, are the building blocks of great palaces. This edifice was built in hate and thus was doomed to fall. Build your palaces on people, on families, on city-states . . . and they will last."

The moral of the story is clear. Structures and organizations are made great by their people infrastructure. Capable, creative, positive, thoughtful people are the fundamental building blocks of strong, surviving organizations. This people infrastructure enables structures and organizations to survive tough and turbulent times. These same human skills will demarcate the great leaders of the next few decades—leaders who will be needed more than ever before.

TWO PREMISES

In keeping with the moral of that Greek tale, two key premises undergird this book:

- The future is the domain of turbulent times.
- The winners of the next decade and beyond will be those who can build people and build teams.

Premise Number 1: The Turbulent Future

While a myriad of factors portend a future far more turbulent than any era of the past, let us focus on seven particular workforce realities that will make managing an organization far more difficult than ever before.

Increased Span of Control

In most organizations, the typical ratio of workers to supervisors has been seven to one. With this ratio, a competent manager could oversee the work in his or her department carefully, yet with relative ease. Direct supervision was a reasonable and manageable task. But in the late 1980s and early 1990s, many organizations extended the span of control to a figure more like twenty to one. Certainly this extension occurred in part to save money. Simultaneously, however, improved communication systems allowed, and in some cases impelled, all parts of the organization to talk with one another more freely. Hence, fewer middle managers were needed—or desired. Businesses lost support staff and middle managers. Moreover, this phenomenon of downsizing was not confined to business and industry. In education, schools lost assistant principals and teachers faced larger classes. Hospital structures became more horizontal and more cost-conscious. The resulting dilemma was that with twenty rather than seven employees to oversee, managers found it more difficult to observe the full range of work. Old strategies of monitoring and control no longer sufficed. Managers became desperate for new and different strategies for supervision.

Changing Work Ethic

In 1957, an opinion poll of adult workers found that the four things most highly valued were the job itself, family, health, and recreation and leisure. Thirty years later, in 1987, a similar survey of adult workers revealed only one difference—but an important one—in value structure. The top four items at that time were family, health, recreation and leisure, and the job itself.

The value of the job had fallen from first place to fourth. While family units are spending significantly more time working for an income than thirty years ago, their valuing of that work has dropped significantly. Consequently, the ability to control someone simply by making the appeal "this is your job" has radically decreased.

It is not that employees do not value work; they do. Rather, the role and value of work has declined relative to other priorities. Since personal health is a higher value than the job, some employees show a greater tendency to use more sick days and comp time than ever before. For others, coaching the Little League team takes priority over staying late at the office. For still others, taking kids to dental appointments or picking them up after school induces stronger allegiance than corporate paperwork. Whatever an individual's new priority, many workers no longer feel their job is their dominant concern. The power of work requirements has eroded greatly. Workers of all sorts and in all kinds of organizations feel they have more options, that they can find alternatives to toxic work conditions. Some observers decry this shift in the job ethic; others applaud it. We do not take sides on that issue but only assert its reality. Authoritative command had a far better chance of success with the work ethic of 1957 than in the climate of 1987. The values of today's workers are far more complex and demanding than they were thirty years ago.

Participative Ethic

One of the megatrends that Naisbitt (1982) has so effectively portrayed is the participative ethic—the desire of those throughout an organization to be involved in decision-making. This value is not posed simply as a desire; rather, it is claimed as a right. The new participative instinct pervades city councils, manufacturing firms, schools, universities, hospitals—all manner of organizations. People want and expect some measure of control over their own destinies.

Nevertheless, a manager should not expect the push for participation to be consistent or predictable. Rather, it will be issue-based and erratic. Most of us desire participation, but without concomitant accountability. We want to tell people what to do and then hold *them* accountable if the idea does not work. While no one would argue that is fair, it is reality—and a reality that managers must face and overcome. Norms, which will be discussed in chapter 3, become critical to surviving this challenge.

Diversity in the Workforce

Just as ethnic, cultural, and family diversity is expanding in the population at large, so too has the workforce become more diverse. Tables 1.1 and 1.2 show the increasing ethnic diversity of the American populace. California, a bellwether state, is experiencing even greater movement toward diversity than the nation as a whole.

Table 1.3 indicates the increasingly complex mix of family structures within the workforce. The American worker is no longer the white Anglo-Saxon Protestant male—he and she are far different from that traditional image. Their needs require more subtle and careful attention. Benefits packages need to be more diverse, management strategies need to be more differentiated, support services need to be broader, and the climate needs to be managed more carefully. A *single*

Table 1.1.   U.S. Ethnicity, 1980, 2000, and 2020 (by percent)

	1980	2000	2020 (projected)
Caucasian	80	72	65
Black	12	13	14
Hispanic	6	11	15
Other	2	4	6

Table 1.2.   California Ethnicity, 1980, 1990, and 2000 (by percent)

	1980	1990	2000
Caucasian	67	58	51
Black	7	7	7
Hispanic	19	25	29
Others	7	10	13

Table 1.3. Women Ages 25 to 54 in the Labor Force (by percent)

	1957	1987
Single Women	80	80
Married Women	33	68
Divorced or Widowed Women	65	79

Source: Futurescan #595, August 1988

strategy might work for highly *homo*geneous populations; *multiple* strategies are necessary for highly *hetero*geneous populations.

Increase in Unsatisfying or Low-Level Jobs

When jobs of the future are described, the words "high-tech," "computerized," "information-oriented," and "futuristic" often appear. Such terms create an exciting, even exhilarating, aura. Alas, the reality falls far short of the claim.

Table 1.4 projects the absolute numbers of new jobs that will be created in the fastest-growing categories. Most of the jobs that are opening up do not require college education and, as now constructed, offer little satisfaction or personal enrichment. Most are service jobs—low in pay and little appreciated in the workforce. As more of our workers engage in these low-paying, "low-tech" jobs, managers find it increasingly important to infuse into these jobs higher degrees of psychic and personal satisfaction and reward. Organizing to capitalize on the participa-

Table 1.4. Projected New Jobs in Fastest-Growing Occupations (1986–2000)

Occupation	Jobs
Sales Clerks	1.2 million
Waiters, Waitresses	752,000
Registered Nurses	612,000
Janitors, Cleaners, Maids	604,000
General Managers and Top Executives	582,000
Cashiers	575,000
Truck Drivers	525,000
General Office Clerks	462,000
Food Counter Workers	449,000
Nursing Aides, Orderlies, Attendants	443,000

Source: U.S. Dept. of Labor Statistics

tive ethic is one means of increasing this sense of investment and satisfaction. That alone, however, will not be enough.

Plateauing Reality

In 1975, there were ten candidates for every middle management opening; in 1985 there were nineteen; in 1995 there were twenty-five. The baby boomers have arrived! They are entering middle age and midcareer. This wonderfully pampered age cohort will now experience the downside of its large size. Adding to this dilemma will be a shortage of middle management positions. Thus, the huge group of baby boomers will try to advance their careers just when career spaces narrow—a larger group, as it were, pressing into a narrowing funnel. Many careers will be blocked, leading in consequence to a plateauing reality—careers split sideways, not upward. In the process, many will leave their organizations while others will simply stay in place, unhappy and resentful. Managing this baby-boom workforce is an intriguing dilemma for the new century.

Recurrent Skill Deficits

Toffler (1980), Cetron (1985), Hodgkinson (1986), and others have detailed the changing skills future workers will need. Some jobs will cease to exist, while the tasks inherent in most others will change significantly. Added to this upheaval is the fact that 13 percent of the workforce is illiterate in English. The manager of the future will train and retrain workers, anticipate and expand job skills, and plan for recurrent skill deficits. In fact, business is already the major educational arena in the United States. In 1989, IBM spent more money on formal and informal training than did Harvard University (table 1.5). Indeed, the total national budget for K–12 education is less than industry spends each year on training. The growing effort to develop and expand skills in the workforce will augment the predicaments faced by the manager of the future.

These are turbulent times. In calm environments, capable management will suffice. In these stormy times, fraught with new perils, a higher order of management is required. Driven by all the factors noted

Table 1.5. Expenditures for Education Compared with Expenditures for Employee Training, 1990

Harvard University's annual budget	$951.7 million
IBM's annual training budget	$1.5 billion
National annual expenditures for K–12 public education	$189.1 billion
Annual employer spending on formal and informal training	$210.0 billion

Source: Futurescan #654, March 1990

above, as well as others you could well recite, the leader of the future must manage with an eye to the future—a future that requires attention to the people infrastructure.

Premise Number 2: A Need to Build Teams

The second premise flows naturally from the first: The winners of the future will be those who can build teams and build people. An increased span of control and a changing work ethic mean that managers can no longer "watch and control" their employees. Workers must be more self-motivated and self-initiating. The increase in low-tech jobs, the participative ethic, and the plateauing reality call on organizations to engender work satisfaction by increasing worker participation in organizational decisions and team responsibility for outcomes.

As the twenty-first century advances, horizontal team structures will replace vertical, authoritarian command structures. The skill deficits and diverse needs of the workforce will demand greater attention to individual growth and change. Workers will not be interchangeable parts of the assembly line, but diverse and individual. People can no longer be viewed as cogs in machinery but must be seen as the main arteries of the organizational body—arteries to be nurtured and strengthened. Consequently, the interaction and interdependence of team members will become critical. Fromm (1991) suggests, "If you want your customer to be treated like a king, treat the people you manage like royalty." Building people builds loyalty in employees and customers!

All these organizational shifts create a new and vastly different reality. Looking to the future, Jamieson and O'Mara argue in their book *Managing Workforce 2000* for four fundamental management skills:

- Matching people and jobs
- Managing and rewarding performance
- Informing and involving people
- Supporting lifestyle and life needs

In essence, they affirm our premises that to survive in the future, to build strong organizations, managers must build strong teams and strong people.

EXPANDING THE FIFTH RESOURCE

Consider the subtitle of this book: "Expanding the Fifth Resource." As you first glanced at the title page, you may have asked yourself, "What is the fifth resource?" Let us start by describing the first four resources. The three classic resources identified in the literature on resource management are

1. People
2. Money
3. Facilities

These are well-established and long-adhered-to bases for fueling organizational achievement. The next resource,

4. Time

has emerged only in the last thirty years, as time has become more limited and precious. We have now become more sensitive to the need for time management. The fifth resource, however, is still too often overlooked. This last resource is

5. Energy

When people have energy—enthusiasm, drive, passion—all the other resources are expanded. People with energy can do more and achieve greater heights than those who lack excitement and commitment and fervor.

Energy expands available money and facilities and time. The converse is even stronger. When we lack energy, we waste people, money, facilities, and time. Energy is the most powerful of all the resources because it expands the others. This book talks about building teams and building people in a way that expands energy, thus enhancing scarce resources. We are asking you—we are *urging* you—to build your organizational future on a foundation of strong, passionate, energized teams and individuals.

BUILDING BLOCKS

It is clear that the management dilemma of the future will call for leaders who can build teams and build people, because only through strong teams and strong people—a "people infrastructure"—will these organizations survive. Of course, almost anyone who reads this book already knows this and values it. The unfortunate reality, however, is that few of us understand the particular building blocks that constitute this people infrastructure. What specifically should we do to build teams and build people? This book is written in response to that question.

It is our belief that rich and effective organizational climates emerge from five building blocks:

1. Creating effective teams
2. Setting norms
3. Managing conflict and politics
4. Endowing people with power
5. Inspiring intrapreneurship

Each of these is, to some degree, interrelated with the others, but each is important on its own. Team-building stresses strategies for welding capable individuals together into an effective and high functioning group. Norm-setting is the key organizational development strategy for moving initial differences into group cohesiveness. Conflict management acknowledges the realities of heterogeneous groups in a turbulent time and provides ways to use inevitable conflicts for organizational health. Empowerment focuses on building the power and strength of individuals. Finally, intrapreneurship is the set of organizational and climate variables that induces enterprising and creative endeavors to emerge and flourish.

When these building blocks are absent, the climate is toxic and, in the long term, will choke and strangle productive work behaviors. The opposite is equally true. When all these building blocks are present, the organizational climate is ripe for productive activity to realize the strategic vision.

ORGANIZATION OF THE BOOK

Each of the following chapters describes the characteristics and dimensions of one of the five building blocks and then concludes with suggestions for pragmatic activities and events that managers can utilize to build that particular dimension. We have written each chapter around lists of components so that the reader will more easily recognize and remember the elements of an effective people infrastructure.

It is not our intent to describe *all* the elements of effective management—that is neither possible nor desirable, or the book would never end. Neither do we mean to offer an academic treatise summing up the array of research on these topics, because those details are unlikely to be used by online managers. Rather, this book is a guidebook to the building blocks of effective team and people management and includes practical suggestions for implementing each of them. We will begin with the two building blocks that focus on group effectiveness: team-building and norm-setting. We will then discuss conflict management as a mechanism for ensuring organizational health and end with the two building blocks that enlarge individual effectiveness and contribution: empowerment and intrapreneurship. Each building block is described as a separate entity that is not welded to the others. In the closing chapter, however, we show how the five blocks fit together into a unit. We explain how to use them with one another, multiplying their effect through synergy to build strong, positive climates. It is our belief that to withstand the storms of the twenty-first century, the new manager must

- Understand the components comprising each building block
- Assess the degree to which each building block exists in his or her organization
- Create activities that overcome climate weakness and enhance climate strengths

Failure to attend to these five building blocks may well doom you to be an artifact of the past. But when you build the teams and build the people in your organization—when you build an edifice on the strengths of the people infrastructure—you build for the future.

CHAPTER 2

Characteristics of Effective Teams

Few managers understand all that is involved in building effective teams. Many believe that team-building consists simply of establishing a "rah-rah" attitude among group members. They envision themselves giving some sort of Knute Rockne speech that fires up the "team" and motivates them for another year's work. In the same vein, we have been called upon on countless occasions to facilitate opening-of-the-year retreats. Typically, the retreat coordinator wants "something motivational." The content is not nearly as relevant as the emotional charge. This is not team-building. This is simply a sugar high that evaporates in the system as quickly as it comes.

Team-building cannot be a one-time event, something you do in September or January with the hope it will last throughout the year. Rather, it is a recurrent and ongoing process of analysis and remediation. Managers need to put aside the mental image of an athletic team and, instead, plan a more structured and systematic approach to building effective teams. While sports have much to teach us about teamwork, they often obscure the realities of managing organizations.

What, then, is team-building? It is not an activity itself, but the result of attending to the characteristics that demarcate effective teamwork. There are seventeen such characteristics. It is the premise of this chapter that the first building block of richer organizational climates is measured by the presence of these characteristics in an organization. When they exist to a high degree, you have an effective team. When they do not, you have a weak team. Moreover, the potency of these characteristics directly impacts the fifth resource, energy. It is the manager's job to assess the strength of these characteristics in the organization and then to address any weaknesses. That is effective team-building.

The remainder of this chapter will describe each of the seventeen characteristics noted in table 2.1. They are organized into four categories:

- Purpose
- Composition
- Interaction
- Structure and Context

We ask you to read on for the sake of your organization. The research has clearly established that organizations that function as teams are significantly more productive and long-lasting. By attending to this first building block, you enhance the achievement and positive climate of your institution.

Table 2.1.   Characteristics of Effective Teams

Purpose
1. Common identity and tenets
2. Common tasks
3. Sense of potency/success

Composition
4. Clear definition of team membership
5. Recognition of individual contributions
6. Balanced roles

Interaction
7. Mutual trust
8. Sense of relationship
9. Open/direct conflict
10. Common base of information
11. High level question-asking and listening
12. Healthy level of stress
13. Toleration of errors
14. Flexibility and responsiveness

Structure and Context
15. Clear understanding/acceptance of group structure
16. Periodic attention to group maintenance
17. Recognition/mitigation of outside forces

PURPOSE

Common Identity and Tenets

Effective teams are purpose-driven. They have someplace they want to go and a hunger to get there. Strong, cohesive groups have a sense of who they are and a clear, definable identity. IBM, Johnson and Johnson, Evanston High School, Princeton University, the town of Williamsburg, Cedars-Sinai Hospital, Bryant Ranch School—to name but a few—have a clear identity and a sense of what brings them together.

One of the more interesting organizations is Mary Kay Cosmetics, which has as its symbol not a pink Cadillac but the bumblebee. The Mary Kay philosophy is "Aerodynamically, the bumblebee shouldn't be able to fly, but the bumblebee doesn't know it so it goes on flying anyway." The Mary Kay company builds their organization on the premise that you must build people's belief in themselves—both as a workforce and a client base. They focus not on what people can*not* do but on what they *can* do.

And the bumblebee is their symbol. The company could have chosen from a myriad of other visual and psychic symbols, but the key question must always be whether a chosen symbol represents the corporate vision. Emblems and logos are of limited use if they do not increase cohesion of purpose.

Another splendid way to explore organizational identity is to establish tenets—belief statements about the organization's raison d'être. The appendix presents several examples of belief statements. There are many names for belief statements—tenets, visions, credos, values—but they all come down to the same thing: a clear statement of belief toward which all members of the organization can work. These statements are not immutable, but they act as guiding stars to organizational direction. When individuals hold in common a sense of where they are heading, they acquire a greater sense of being a team. Vision and tenets provide that collective consciousness.

Common Tasks

To be a cohesive team, groups need common tasks—things they do together. Groups without jobs to do together might be congenial, fun, or dynamic, but they cannot form teams because nothing necessitates their long-term cooperation. A family parallel lies in the reality that a common point for divorce is the first two years after the last child leaves home. The couple has stayed together because they have had a common job—raising the children. When the children leave, the couple may find they have nothing left in common, nothing they must do with one another—and they separate.

Groups lacking a common task are simply involved in parallel play; they do the same thing, not together, but side by side. Teachers exemplify this circumstance. They do similar jobs, but they work independently of each other. Often, the teachers' association is the only setting in which teachers necessarily share tasks. Thus, the reason teachers often have difficulty forming cohesive teams is that they lack common tasks. Lawrence and Lorsch (1969) vividly describe the nature of both differentiation and integration. Without common tasks, the latter variable seldom occurs.

In one company we worked with, neither the management team nor members of respective departments had ever met together in groups. Each person had been given individual assignments and had continued to work in that manner. Because no sense of "team" existed within the organization, finger-pointing was rampant. If shipments of the end product were late, the fault always lay with another person or department. Dramatizing their common task of turning out the best product on the market began the process of team formation. When we created cross-functional task groups, we began to build a strong sense of team.

A vision for the organization describes a common task for all its members. The appendix includes sample vision statements that give team members a sense of direction—a sense that people are in it together for a worthwhile purpose. A vision of the future has emerged as one of the most important characteristics of effective enterprises in both the public and the private sectors.

As you examine people in your organization, notice what they do together. What common tasks do they share? If your answer is "very few," then you may have an enjoyable group but only limited capacity to develop a team.

Sense of Potency/Success

Groups that are convinced that they are successful or that they have the capacity to succeed act as cohesive teams. The converse is even stronger. Group members who believe that they are failures or lack the capacity to succeed actually turn on one another. They look for scapegoats; they point fingers; they look for other groups with which to associate.

As noted in previous writing:

> [A key] precondition for unfreezing is *potency*—you can change only if you believe you can. . . . If someone wants to teach me tennis, and I demur that I am too slow or too fat or too old or too anything, then I guarantee I will never learn tennis. If you say you can't fight City Hall, then you can't. If you say to your spouse, "That's just the way I am. You married me that way. I can't change," then you won't. If you say, "You can't teach an old dog new tricks," then the dog will remain safe and comfortable with his old tricks. A splendid old adage says:
>
> > *If you say you can,*
> > *or if you say you cannot,*
> > *you are right.* (Harvey 1990)

Change occurs only if people believe they have the power to change.

People who believe in themselves can accomplish much. Success is a keystone to creating that sense of self-worth. As the saying goes, "Nothing breeds success like success." When you focus on what people can*not* do, that is what you get—nothing done.

To illustrate this point, I recall my children's sports experience. John had a Little League coach who pointed out every mistake a kid made. The coach called the entire team together at practice and emphasized how John or one of his "teammates" had done the wrong thing. He was well-meaning, but he had those kids so scared of making a mistake that they tried very little. Conversely, I remember John's Jaycee basketball coach, Bob Dyer. Each kid was a winner, and each kid played. There was one boy, Joey, who was strong and lively and not much else. Bob convinced him that he "owned" the basketball on rebounds. Joey went after rebounds with a verve like no other, and he led our team in rebounds (and fouls). Bob convinced him he was a winner with an important role in the team.

Successful managers find ways to elevate the successes of others, to make everyone believe in the potency of the group. Sometimes, however, recognition of achievement can be done with an eye not to building but to punishment. We had a client who loved clean workstations in his shop, but his men seldom complied. One day he walked into his shop and saw a new man, Mike, at his impeccable workstation. So he called everyone together.

"Hey, look at Mike's station," he told them. "This is great. Look how clean it is. Why aren't you other clowns more like Mike? Great job, Mike. Hey, guys, take note! This is the way it ought to be done."

A week later he went back into his shop, and guess what? That's right! Mike's station was a mess. The rest of the workers were angry and felt shown up. Mike's choices were to comply with them or be ostracized. The manager was mad at the men, but he should have been mad at himself. He used recognition to punish others, not to celebrate success.

Positive environments that emphasize success foster success. The messages you send are often the messages you get back. If you want to build a strong team, you need to send them messages that they can succeed, have succeeded, and will continue to succeed. While such messages are never sufficient to drive success, they are necessary.

COMPOSITION

Clear Definition of Team Membership

To many of you, team membership may seem a wholly unnecessary characteristic—surely it is obvious who constitutes the group! However, in our experience, team membership may not be clear at all. When we ask "management team" members to list independently the members of the management team, we often get lists with different sets of names. Sometimes people even omit their own names. They feel they are not "true" members of the group, just observers.

If a group is to function as a team, its members must share a clear and explicit knowledge of the persons who are and are not part of the group. When the boundaries are unclear—when individuals are some-times in, sometimes out—then the group is less a team and more an arena for discussion.

Among the attributes of membership is an expectation that everyone will attend and participate. To be part of a team, you need to be there and be active. "Active membership" may be defined differently for dif-ferent people, but all must perceive that no member is marginal, unim-portant, or parasitic.

Recognition of Individual Contributions

In effective teams, each person has a role and everyone knows what that role is. There are two aspects to this important characteristic. The first defines the skills and contributions each person brings to the team. Individuals who feel they bring nothing to the group will, indeed, man-ifest a like contribution to team progress—nothing. Not everyone's skill or contribution will be the same, but each must provide something of worth. In chapter 6 we will speak again of the strength-bombard-ment exercise, in which each group member in turn receives praise from each of the others. This is but one way to affirm individual strengths. Role-analysis technique (described in chapter 4) is another. No matter how it is accomplished, each team member must perceive that he or she is of worth, bringing something important to the progress of the team.

The second aspect of this characteristic recognizes publicly the important role of each member. Too often this recognition is implicit. We assume that the other person knows what she brings to the group. Do not make this assumption. Instead, explicitly state the roles and skills of team members. With that validation, members are more likely to replicate these roles and to produce positive outcomes. A most won-drous, yet simple, phrase is "I need you." When people feel *un*needed, they are likely to remain passive or even to act destructively. When people feel needed, they act positively. Moreover, the skills of team members are needed by the team itself, not merely by the manager. Therefore, good managers make explicit their statement of need as well as ensure that such expressions are mutual among team members.

My father once shared his experience while working as a supervisor for Sears, Roebuck and Co., then one of the largest mail-order houses in the United States. One day the manager called together the members of his department. As they entered the room, my father was spotted with a handmade cardboard sign around his neck. It stated simply, "Tell me why I'm needed." The other members spontaneously began sharing why they needed him. As my father tells it, he walked out of that meeting six feet off the ground with a clear notion of what he brought to the team. But that was not the end of it. That roughly drawn sign was seen for months, each time around the neck of different employees.

Balanced Roles

Imagine a Roman trireme with hundreds of oars and only three people rowing. It would not travel very far, if it moved at all. But we do exactly that in many organizations. Schools are classic examples. We have hundreds of tasks to do and we give them to the same three teachers. We know that Maureen, Dac, and Joy are wonderful task achievers, so we give them each new job that comes along until we burn them out or, figuratively speaking, kill them. Effective organizations, on the other hand, spread out the tasks, giving each person a "piece of the action."

Balancing roles, of course, increases *im*perfection, since a job cannot always be assigned to the person who does it best. As you spread roles around, you have less competent people doing more things. This outcome violates the task-achiever's very premise for being—perfection. But that compromise is a necessary evil, tolerated for the sake of long-term organizational health.

If you do not balance roles, those less-skilled employees never have the experience or potency to increase their skills. "They don't need me. Maureen or Dac or Joy will do it," people say to themselves. But consider: We all began as apprentices and made mistakes. That is how we grew. Managers who limit participation to a few or focus important work on a limited number of workers diminish individual strength and undercut team consciousness. Strong teams have everyone pulling at the oars, side by side, despite the fact that some members are stronger than others.

The importance of this characteristic of teams was confirmed in forming and opening a new school. The tasks were plentiful. Many new staff members had been added to the small initial planning group. The principal's first tendency was to hand a task to the person she knew could complete it most efficiently. Rejecting that inclination, she assigned equally important tasks to each. Sometimes they fumbled, but mostly they succeeded—maybe not the way the principal would have done it, but effectively just the same. The results soon manifested themselves when everyone felt they had a piece of the action. They were certain they could "try" things and would succeed.

INTERACTION

Mutual Trust

Trust is much like love—we know it when we see it, but we are not sure what creates it. Trust is not an act or set of acts but the result of other actions or variables. We suggest five conditions that account for trust and discuss each in order of importance.

Interdependence

When I need you and you need me, we have a basis for trust. When I need you but you do *not* need me, you can be arbitrary and capricious and at some point probably will be. The adverse is equally true. Only when we have mutual need can trust evolve.

Think of the phrase spoken between couples, "You take me for granted." This is simply another way of saying that you do not demonstrate your need for me. A task sociogram is one way of assessing this condition in an organizational setting. Working with a group of five to ten, you ask everyone, "Who do you need to get your job done?" Then you look for mutual two-way transactions—pairs of people who say they need each other. The more two-way transactions in a group, the higher the capacity for trust. The more one-way transactions, the lower the probabilities of trust. The more we need each other, both in reality and in perception, the more we can build trust.

Consistency

Research shows that people trust those who are consistent from word to deed and from deed to deed. Of these two, the former is most important—"I can count on you to do what you say." In a colloquial phrase, you "walk the talk." Much disillusionment with politicians reflects their inconsistency between word and deed. In the battle to win, politicians promise much, but in the face of reality, they deliver little. They talk about cutting back and then give themselves pay raises.

Contrast such politicians with one of our small-business clients facing the recession of Christmas 1990. This businessman told his employees there would be reductions and cutbacks—and he started by cutting his own salary 25 percent and dropping all his club memberships. Those actions sent a message that he was serious and could be trusted to experience the same shortfalls as everyone else. Later, when business improved, he did not restore his benefits until everyone else's benefits were in place. He modeled what he asked of others. Other examples are university deans who talk of academic priorities and then teach regularly to show their commitment. Or elementary school principals who are regularly visible on the playground, at the bus stop, and in classrooms. Behavior needs to be consistent with verbal priorities. When you act in ways that say your words can be trusted, you enrich the entire climate of the organization.

Honesty

People who lie, cheat, and double-deal are simply not trusted. You can get away with these behaviors in the short run, but in the long run duplicitous actions become widely known. You cannot hide this kind of light under a basket. Dishonesty can involve both commission and omission. Telling lies is not the only form of dishonesty; forgetting to mention the truth is also dishonest. When you are known to be honest and committed to integrity, you build trust.

Affability

Likable people are easier to trust. Affability supports trusting relationships. To be likable is not sufficient, however, although some leaders foolishly try to build trust solely on that basis. The manager who walks around being "one of the group" but is without substance may be well liked—but is not apt to be trusted on the professional level necessary to build effective teams. Likewise, colleagues or managers who persistently express negative attitudes and whine about everything are hard to relate to. I worked for a university president who whined and moaned about all the catastrophes about to befall us. In the process, he was trying to set himself up as the university's savior. All he accomplished was to make himself the least-liked and least-trusted person on campus. Affability, though only fourth on this list, does still contribute to trusting, positive relationships.

Extension of Trust

There is an old but true aphorism that says "Those who give trust, get trust." When you send messages to colleagues that you will give trust only when they "deserve" it, you set up cautious and untrusting relationships. No, this is not a Pollyanna world in which everyone is loving and nice. When you extend trust, you may well be violated. You need to anticipate such eventualities and think through in your own mind what you will do when they occur. But if you avoid extending trust for fear of violation, you will then be a double victim—they will have achieved their purpose and you will have gained nothing at all. Your fear of giving trust will make you a less-trusted person. Remember: The messages you send are the messages you receive—those who give trust, get trust.

When these five conditions—interdependence, consistency, honesty, affability, and extension of trust—are present, the soil is fertile for trust. This equation is not perfectly predictive, but the probability is high that when these five conditions exist, trust does also. With trust, you have a richer organizational climate.

Sense of Relationship

Joy*ful* environments are more productive than joy*less* environments. When individuals understand each other as people and have the opportunity to enter into relationships, they feel more like colleagues and team members. All those potlucks and staff parties and retreats and recognition lunches and TGIF gatherings are important to team-building. As with affability, they are not sufficient, but they are necessary. Sociability fosters interpersonal commitment. When I care about you as a person, I am more likely to work with you as a team member. A dilemma arises if some group members attempt to supplant organizational goals with sociability. Such employees come to work for the sake of relationships, not to achieve organizational purpose. Nevertheless, although relationships must be balanced with purpose, those organizations that propel commitment through joy are more productive than organizations dedicated solely to task.

Open or Direct Conflict

A small school district in northern California invited us to help them with team-building. When we asked the superintendent about the strengths of the district, he said, "We never fight; we don't conflict." To that we replied, "That's exactly why you need team-building." Teams with no open conflict are dying entities. Not that you ought to engage in open warfare, but groups who have any vitality at all, any ideas, any instincts for growth will have conflicts. All vital families have conflicts, as do all vital corporations, schools, colleges, and hospitals. Where there are creative, excited people, conflicts arise. The challenge is to keep these conflicts open and public so the team can take responsibility for resolving them.

Hidden conflicts fester. Therefore, apparent peace should be recurrently examined. It may be a sign that previous conflicts have been successfully resolved, but it might also mean that open conflict is not legitimized in the organization. The latter situation reduces the level of satisfaction and interferes with team operations. Research by Drolet (1992) found that conflict norms are necessary to satisfaction with an organization's operating system. The stronger the norms that support productive conflict, the higher the level of satisfaction. Do your employees feel they can confront each other when conflict arises? If conflict seems absent, ask yourself whether it might be submerged.

Common Base of Information

I went to a meeting one time and the group began to discuss a memo the vice president had sent out the previous Tuesday. But I had never received a copy of the memo, so I asked about it. The VP replied, "We didn't send you one because it really doesn't affect you." That memo, which, had I received it, I probably would have thrown away as unimportant now became the most important piece of "information" in my life. That memo no longer signified information; now it stood for inclusion. I wanted to be equal with everyone else.

Access to information communicates importance and inclusion. Very often, as efficient managers, we send out information only on an "as needed" basis. If information were only information, that procedure would work, but in teams all members have a right to know—indeed, a necessity to feel included and respected. A common phrase these days is "out of the loop." When you are "out of the loop," you are out of power; you are a less-than-equal member in a group of equals. So on matters of import to the team, share all information with all team members. They may not need that memo to do their job, but they may need it to feel part of the team. When in doubt, include.

High-Level Question-Asking and Listening

Upon analyzing the discourse of most business meetings, we have found that only 4 to 5 percent of the utterances are questions or answers to questions. The rest of the verbalizations are statements. Incidentally, these findings are fairly consistent with Bellack's (1966) research on teacher discourse. Few of us ask questions; most of us prefer to tell. Effective teams, on the other hand, are characterized by questioning and listening behaviors. One hears

"What is the problem?"
"What do you think we should do?"
"What would work best?"
"What are the alternatives?"
"What are the consequences if we do it that way?"

"Why do you think it will work best that way?"
"Who ought to be involved?"
"What deadline should we set?"

The questions are endless. But the more you ask them of one another and then listen to the responses, the more you act as a team. If you want a productive team, focus on asking questions. Questioning is not only more empathetic and inclusive, it is also more efficient. Groups that use high levels of question-asking and listening shorten their decision-making time by about 30 percent. If you want to go fast, ask; if you want to go slow, tell.

Healthy Level of Stress

Stress is one of the more misunderstood realities of productive organizations and individuals. Obviously, settings with extremely high levels of stress are counterproductive. If you have eighteen hours' work to do in eight and all of it must be done today, you cannot flourish or work effectively. The stress imposed by the system will overwhelm you. You will either leave or look for niches within which to hide, niches such as "That's not my job," or "I know nothing about it," or "I did my part."

However, the other end of the continuum is equally problematic. Organizations or individuals with no stress will fail to grow or create. An old adage proclaims "Necessity is the mother of invention." This truism could just as easily (but not as lyrically) be restated as, "Stress is the mother of growth and creativity." Implied is another reason for the importance of conflict to organizations—it sparks new ideas and possibilities. Now let us be clear. Stress does not feel good. If you go home at night and say, "Darling, what a great day this was. We had so much stress!" then we know you are not playing with a full deck. But do recognize the importance of moderate stress as a progenitor of ideas and possibilities even as you recognize that stress pitched too high *or* too low is unhealthy for teams.

An intriguing body of research comes to mind as an extension of this principle. Barker (1968) examined the notion of "manning"—the optimal number of people to get the job done. He postulated three conditions:

Undermanned: too few people for the tasks to be accomplished
Optimally manned: exactly the right number of people for the tasks to be accomplished
Overmanned: too many people for the tasks to be accomplished

He found that the most unproductive of the three conditions was "overmanned." Some bureaucratic governmental agencies exemplify overmanned, hence underproductive, organizations. His most interesting conclusion, however, was that the most productive condition was "undermanned," not "optimally manned." When there were too few people to get the job done, everyone had to take more responsibility and initiative. Necessities forced efficiencies. Undermanned settings create much stress but also more productivity and, ultimately, more satisfaction with what is accomplished. In undermanned settings, I am needed more. That is why privatized governmental services work so well. In my years as an elected official, I have consistently found that public services contracted to private agencies are more effective and cost efficient than the same services conducted by public-sector organizations. This is true of everything from trash-hauling to golf-course management. The public sector optimally mans at high wages; the private sector undermans at lower wages combined with incentive clauses. Organizations that manage stress, allowing it to range neither too high nor too low, induce creative, productive teamwork.

Toleration of Errors

Suppose a manager turns to one of his workers and encourages him to be innovative by saying: "I want you to be on the cutting edge. I want you to create products that no one has ever thought of before. I want you to be risk-taking and innovative. And if you make a mistake, I'll have your neck!" Will the worker tend to remember "innovative" and "risk-taking"—or will the words "I'll have your neck" stick in his mind? The answer is obvious. When we seek creative, new opportunities, we must be prepared for mistakes. Organizations claiming to be "error free" do not spark their employees to innovation or risk-taking; instead, they are toxic, choking off ventures that involve any risk.

A couple of true anecdotes effectively illustrate this critical principle. Bennis and Nanus (1985) tell the story of Tommy Watson at IBM. One of his employees lost $25 million for IBM and submitted his resignation to Watson. Watson called him in and asked why he was resigning, to which the employee replied, somewhat quizzically, "Because I lost us $25 million." Watson's response was, "If you leave us, we lose $25 million; if you stay, we have $25 million worth of learning." For the leader of IBM, the issue was not the mistake but learning from it.

A second story that also illustrates this tolerance of error is told of Johnny Major, the Tennessee football coach who directed his volunteer football team to the 1991 Sugar Bowl and who, decades before, in 1956, had been second in Heisman Trophy voting as a tailback for the same University of Tennessee volunteers. As it happened, in the 1957 Sugar Bowl, star runner Major had fumbled a punt that led to Baylor's winning touchdown. After the game, as Major's mother was en route to visiting the locker room, reporters caught her and asked her feelings about the fumble that lost Tennessee the Sugar Bowl title. Her reply: "Even I burn the biscuits on occasion." She did not apologize, she did not blame. She simply accepted the reality of error. No doubt that mental strength also pervaded Major and made him the man he was—not error free, just willing to persevere and to learn from mistakes. If we had more leaders who could say "Even I burn the biscuits on occasion," we would have more organizations stretching to splendid heights. Research referred to earlier (Drolet 1992) identifies risk-taking as one of two predictors of satisfaction with an organization's operating system. Organizations whose norms encouraged innovation without fear of reprisal—places where "Your job is mine" was not used as a threat—showed higher employee satisfaction. And the higher the satisfaction, the more energy is available to meet the goals of the organization.

Flexibility and Responsiveness

Whether we like it or not, the world approaching the twenty-first century is an open-systems world. A closed system is one that receives its input and direction from within the system itself. A closed system works well in a stable, predictable environment. An open system is one that receives its input and direction from both within and without the system, with the majority of direction coming from without. Open systems survive well in turbulent, volatile environments.

Farming traditionally exemplified a closed system. I grew up on a farm, and we always planted what we had planted the year before. We always assumed the soil would be the same and that the needs of the area would remain constant. Farmers like us did not survive as the soil eroded and the marketplace changed. We never looked at other techniques or advances; we simply looked inside our traditional system and took direction from it. Railroads through the middle of this century also illustrate closed systems in an increasingly turbulent world. Many universities, too, seem oblivious to societal changes that will ultimately break into their supposedly closed systems.

IBM, on the other hand, is an excellent example of an open system. They scanned the environment, saw the changes coming, and responded accordingly. Our university, the University of La Verne, is also a good example. It went from a staid, dying small undergraduate college to a creative, experimenting, comprehensive university in a matter of one decade. The faculty and administration stopped asking one another what to do and began to examine the needs and values of the changing student base. The organization was flexible and responsive.

In an open system, however, errors are inevitable. There is more stress and discomfort. But those down sides must not deter a manager from looking beyond the organization. A closed system in an open-systems world is akin to a frog in a cool pan of water on a stove. When the burner is turned on underneath the pan, the frog will stay in the pan until it is boiled to death. Comfort may be enticing, but before you know it, you are dead! Strong, positive teams scan their environment and possess the flexibility and responsiveness that enable them to change.

STRUCTURE AND CONTENT

Clear Understanding/Acceptance of Group Structure

There is no one right way to structure a team. There are plenty of wrong ways, but no one right way. Whatever the structure, the important issues are:

1. Does everyone understand the structure?
2. Does everyone accept this structure?

The key factor in any structure is buy-in by the members. Vertical or horizontal, leaderless, collaborative or authoritarian—any structure can work if team members value the structure and understand and accept their role in it. When individuals feel unfulfilled in the group structure or do not understand it or do not accept their role in it, that is when structures fail. Some structures are easier avenues to productive organizational climates—collaborative, horizontal structures, for instance—but all forms can work and do work, as long as members are committed to them.

Periodic Attention to Group Maintenance

Mushrooms are the strangest of organisms; they grow best in the dark. So, too, do rumor, innuendo, enmity, greed, and spite. When we hide these organization plagues, when we keep them in the dark, they grow and prosper. Open discourse diminishes rumors and innuendo. Honest expression of feelings limits enmity, greed, and spite. Consequently, a key strategy for positive team climate is a periodic "time out." During these pauses, the team turns from its tasks to attend to group function in order to debrief feelings and understandings among group members. The purpose of a work team is not the same as that of a T group (therapy group) or a social club, but effective task achievement does require sensitivity to the feelings of team members. No matter how careful you are as a leader, no matter how trusting the established environment, misunderstandings and minor slights do occur. Catch them while they are small so they can evaporate and the climate can remain rich.

Recognition/Mitigation of Outside Forces

One characteristic of an effective leader is pragmatism (Yukl 1981; Stogdill 1974). Leaders who are realistic about their possibilities are significantly more likely to achieve their objectives. This realism needs to run in both directions, however. Effective leaders must also understand and assess the limitations, the givens, they face—whether budgetary, political, interpersonal, or legislative. Otherwise, disillusionment will set in when team efforts collide head on with these barriers. Disillusioned people achieve little.

Conversely, a leader cannot be too limiting. A manager must not suppose limitations that do not truly exist or achievements will be unduly constrained. Playing it safe is just as faulty as playing the Pollyanna. The middle ground is where effective leaders—and effective teams—operate. Strong, productive teams make a careful and honest assessment of their environment. They know the givens and are realistic about their potential achievements. They do not trust those who say, "The world is your oyster; you can do anything you want." They know that not everything is possible.

To be overly sanguine is an error; to be overly pessimistic is an error. Not to look at all is another mistake. Paradoxically, when the givens are left unexplored, people assume parameters that are far more restrictive than reality. Figure 2.1 represents the magnitude of difference between the two conditions.

ASSESSING TEAM CHARACTERISTICS

As noted earlier, team-building involves first understanding those characteristics that define effective teams, then assessing their existence in

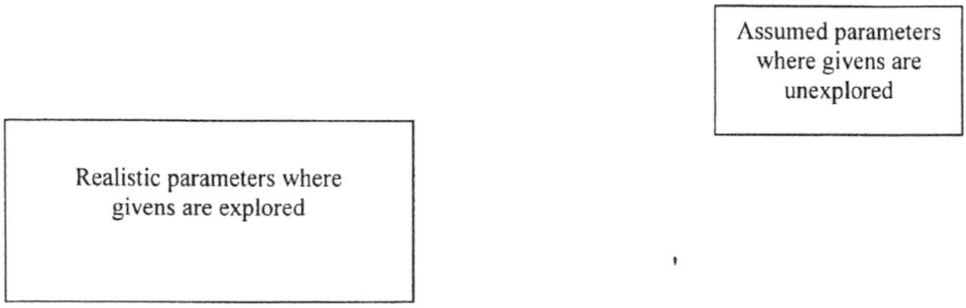

Realism expands parameters, reduces potential disillusionment, and creates more productive teams.

Figure 2.1   Operating Parameters for Problem Solving

your organization, and, finally, doing something about those that are weak. Table 2.2 displays a survey form we use for such an assessment. After explaining the characteristics, we usually have group members rate each characteristic individually. We then divide the total group into subgroups of five to ten and ask the subgroups to arrive at a rating. This rating should represent consensus, not simple averaging. We allow forty-five minutes for this step, then ask each group to report out their ratings, variable by variable. A typical team of forty-five, working in six subgroups, might have a data display something like table 2.3.

Chapin School District is led by a hard-driving, high-achievement superintendent who does little to attend to group feelings or perceptions. This profile, with its strengths in identity and clear roles and its weaknesses in mutual trust and tolerance of error, is fairly typical of such a superintendent.

The other interesting set of variables consists of those that show a significant split in scores (more than one apart): sense of relationship,

Table 2.2. Survey of Team Characteristics

Our team has:

	Not at all		Somewhat		Very much
Common identity/tenets	1	2	3	4	5
Common tasks	1	2	3	4	5
Sense of potency/success	1	2	3	4	5
Clear membership	1	2	3	4	5
Clear roles	1	2	3	4	5
Balanced roles	1	2	3	4	5
Mutual trust	1	2	3	4	5
Sense of relationship	1	2	3	4	5
Open conflict	1	2	3	4	5
Common information	1	2	3	4	5
Effective questioning/listening	1	2	3	4	5
Healthy stress	1	2	3	4	5
Acceptance of error	1	2	3	4	5
Flexibility/responsiveness	1	2	3	4	5
Accepted group structure	1	2	3	4	5
Attention to group maintenance	1	2	3	4	5
Recognition of outside forces	1	2	3	4	5

Strengths: Weaknesses:

Table 2.3. Survey of Team Characteristics (Chapin School District)

Our team has:

	Not at all 1	2	Somewhat 3	4	Very much 5
Common identity/tenets						‖	‖|
Common tasks				‖‖			
Sense of potency/success	‖		‖				
Clear membership				‖‖			
Clear roles				‖‖			
Balanced roles		‖	‖	‖	
Mutual trust	‖‖	‖			
Sense of relationship	‖			‖	‖
Open conflict	‖‖				
Common information			‖‖				
Effective questioning/listening			‖‖				
Healthy stress	‖		‖	‖	
Acceptance of error	‖‖	‖			
Flexibility/responsiveness				‖‖			
Accepted group structure			‖‖‖		
Attention to group maintenance	‖‖|				
Recognition of outside forces			‖‖				

Strengths:	Common identity	Weaknesses:	Mutual trust
	Clear understanding of who is part of the team		Open/direct conflict
	Clear roles		Tolerance of error
	Flexibility/responsiveness		Attention to group maintenance

balanced roles, and healthy stress. Such splits are also typical of organizations that have in-groups, particularly cliques of members who have been entrenched for a long time. The in-group sees relationships as positive and roles as balanced, but the new people feel left out.

What do you do about such a profile? Team-building events for each of the four sections (purpose, composition, interaction, and structure and context) are provided in the following pages. This chapter concludes with a prescription for Chapin School District.

A SHORTENED MODEL

While all seventeen variables add to our ability to predict teamness, ten factors out of the seventeen seem to be the most important in predicting teamness (Corkrum 1996). They are:

- Mutual trust
- Common tasks
- Awareness/acceptance and group structure
- Open/direct conflict
- Risk-taking
- Awareness of external environment
- Common identity/tenets
- Sense of relationship
- High level of listening and question-asking
- Periodic attention to group maintenance

Corkrum even reports that "five fast ID Elements" to predict teamness are:

- Common tasks
- Mutual trust
- Open direct conflict
- Risk-taking
- Awareness of group structure

And he further reports,

> In summary, team building is nothing more than an on-going program of assessing and attending to the seventeen functional characteristics of effective teams. The abbreviated versions will build a utilitarian acceptance of the construct and answer confidence in its practical application to an array of work groups.

In other words, it's valid to see all seventeen variables, but if you haven't got the time or you want to make a quick assessment, use the ten-factor version or even the five-factor version.

TEAM-BUILDING EVENTS

Purpose

- Establish a common identity and common tenets
- Set common tasks
- Cultivate a sense of potency/success

Constructing Tenet/Value Statements (See Examples in Appendix)

Tenets are fundamental, operational principles that govern the direction of the organization's programs and plans. They establish the focus through which programs, products, and processes should be filtered prior to any decision. Tenets are usually comprised of seven to ten statements of principle that drive the organization.

Without a strong belief in common tenets, values, or guiding principles, it is difficult for a team to flourish. Developing these belief statements takes time and talking. With a facilitator, use the following process:

1. Begin with each member of the team determining four to six of the organization's beliefs from the individual's perspective.
2. Place the team members in pairs to share their individual beliefs and come to consensus on six of the beliefs.
3. Form groups of four team members and repeat step 2.
4. Post the results of each group.
5. Have members place like beliefs together.
6. Discuss if these are true beliefs held by all.
7. Come to consensus on the eight to ten beliefs that will guide your organization.

Creating a Vision Statement (See Examples in Appendix)

A vision statement is future-oriented. It describes what the organization is to look like and how it will successfully fulfill its intents. A vision statement is an outgrowth of the organization's tenets. In portraying a future state, the vision statement sketches clients, services, and strategies. It is the focus on the horizon that all members of the organization keep in sight and constantly work toward.

Attributes of a Vision:

1. It focuses on a better future.
2. It encourages hopes and dreams.

3. It appeals to common values.
4. It states positive outcomes.
5. It emphasizes the strength of a unified group.
6. It uses word pictures, images, and metaphors.
7. It communicates enthusiasm and kindles excitement.

What a Vision Is Not:

1. A mission statement
2. A simple statement of what is
3. Boring and unimaginative
4. Written but not used

What Is Included in a Vision Statement

1. Desired Future State—What does your organization want to look like five years from now?
2. Clientele Served—Do you want to change who you are currently serving? Do you want to expand or retract from the current clientele?
3. Services Provided—Do you want to redesign current general services, such as providing adult education, offering continual professional development, introducing cutting-edge technology, or offering global services?
4. Major Strategies—Often confused with number 3, these are more specific in nature. Do you want every member of the team to have the opportunity to individualize professional development? Do you want to offer specific leadership possibilities?

Norm-Setting (See Chapter 3)

Norms are the behaviors widely accepted by people in the organization. Norms exist in an organization whether they are identified or not, so a wise manager takes time to reach consensus on a set of norms and writes them down where they are seen by all. The next chapter describes the norm-setting process in detail.

Organizational Logo

An organization is linked with its symbol. Schools have mascots, businesses have discernible visuals (e.g., the apple). A logo lets others know who you are. It gives team members a common image, identity, and representation of their organization.

Organizational Motto

A motto or slogan communicates what you are about. For instance, the slogan "Reflect the Past, Explore the Present, and Invent the Future" depicts an organization on the move but one that is taking advantage of lessons learned from experience. Your motto should embody your shared efforts and focus.

Organizational Symbols

Symbols reflect a shared identity as well as organizational purpose. They visualize and strengthen the bonding of the team. Think of a major league sports team without a common uniform or symbol. Would they be as prominent? as recognizable? Organizational symbols allow members of a team to show their pride in working for the organization.

Appropriate Task Forces

Task forces bring together team members with varied skills and expertise to address a common task. Members of a task force share strengths and ideas as they problem-solve together. They invest time and energy in completing a specific assignment. They usually work closely together for an intense period of time and then dissolve. The strength of the task force structure lies in its ability to resolve a complex problem even as it empowers its members.

Team Training Sessions

A sense of bonding occurs when an entire team participates in staff training. Team members acquire common language and concepts. To maximize team-building efforts, we strongly encourage that these training sessions take place away from the work site.

Regular Department/Team Meetings

Regular meetings result in a common base of information, stronger working relationships, and an understanding of each member's interdependence with the others. Doyle and Straus have written an excellent book entitled *How to Make Meetings Work* (Berkeley, 1986) that is a resource all managers need.

Celebrations

Getting together to celebrate successes and project completions and to welcome new members not only provides shared personal experiences but also, and more important, brings joy and laughter to the team.

Celebrations do not need to be elaborate to work. Calling together the team to congratulate them for success or highlighting the specific member for results can occur in the break room or at a central location. Beginning staff meetings with time to congratulate each other on a success of the week is a way to make celebrations intrinsic to the organizational procedures.

Awards and Recognition (See Chapter 7)

Recognition and awards take on many styles. The important point is, DO IT! People thrive on recognition. They are empowered to move forward and reach for new vistas each time their efforts are singled out. Nothing succeeds like success. People who are recognized are energized. Energy is that important fifth resource requiring continual cultivation by managers.

- Clear Definition of Team Membership
- Recognition of Individual Contributions
- Balance Roles

Formal Identification of Team Members

Each time a team is formed or changes, identifying who is on the team is an important issue. Does everyone know who is on the team? Have each member write out a list of who *he or she* thinks is on the team. Check to see if the member was included on his or her own list. You may be surprised at the omissions, especially in large or physically disjointed organizations. For example, schools often have trouble identifying "the team." Does it include teachers only or instructional assistants as well? What about the custodian? Clearly define the team for all to know.

Photographic Display of the Team

Once the team is identified, everyone should know who they are. Post their pictures in the lobby or common work area. You might even write a short biographical or work-skill sketch for each member. Advertise your team!

Strength Bombardment (See Chapter 7)

Strength bombardment is a simple exercise that lets people know what they bring to the team. Periodically, at the end of a meeting, ask all the members to concentrate on one person. Let each person share that individual's strengths and skills. With a small team (six to eight), all members could be targeted in a single strength-bombardment session as each member is taken in turn. Allow approximately forty-five minutes for a team this size.

"Balanced Roles" Checklist

The Balanced Roles checklist ensures that tasks are evenly distributed—that growth, and therefore empowerment, activities are available to all members of the team. By the same token, balancing roles prevents burnout of a few. Keep the checklist handy and refer to it each time you must give a new assignment.

Assign extra duties equitably. Base assignment on strengths or pos-

sible strengths of team members. The Balanced Roles checklist is helpful not only to assign tasks; it can also track timelines to prevent
overlapping of important or broad duties.

Easy Tasks				Complex Tasks
1	2	3	4	5
Nancy	Tim	Maria	Jose	Andy
Distribute and	Investigate	Tabulate	Manage	Interface with
Collect Staff	Retreat Sites	Surveys	Problem-Solving	Complaints from
Survey			Council	Clients
	Nancy			Jose
	Coordinate			New Project
	Team Socials			

1. Place each team member's name in an appropriate cell with the
   task that person has been assigned.

- For example, Nancy has been asked to distribute and collect a staff
  survey. This is an easy task for her to accomplish.
- Jose has been asked to provide leadership in the Problem-Solving
  Council. This is a relatively complex task.
- Andy has been asked to interface with unhappy clients and to
  come to some kind of resolution of complaints. This is a highly
  complex task.
- Jose has also been asked to coordinate the biggest project in the
  organization's history. Quite a complex job.
- Tim has been directed to investigate possible sites for the organization's retreat. While it may not be an easy task, it certainly is not
  complex.
- Nancy will be coordinating team socials. This is a fairly easy task.
- Maria has been asked to tabulate the staff survey and put the
  results in a format for distribution. This task is probably the middle
  range of difficulty.

2. As you can begin to see, Jose carries the much more complex
   tasks for the organization. The questions then become: Is this fair

for his job description? Are other team member's skills being used? Are they being asked to grow or stagnate?

Another Balanced-Roles Checklist

Name	Task	Difficulty
		1 = Easy/5 = Complex
John	Attend meeting with boss and important client	4
	Organize staff retreat	5
Scott	Work with task force to design new logo and image	5
	Attend public meetings with city council	3
Andy	Work with team grievances	5
	Play on softball team	2

In this situation, the team tasks are fairly balanced. Each member has a complex and easier task assigned. The closer the balance, the stronger the team and the better the outcomes.

Team Meals

Eating together provides a bon vivant spirit. It allows members to relax and talk without an agenda. These informal times often give birth to a new idea or the solution to a pressing problem. Do not overlook the importance of these social times together!

INTERACTION

- Mutual trust
- Sense of relationship
- Open and direct conflict
- Common base of information
- High-level question-asking and listening

- Healthy level of stress
- Toleration of errors
- Flexibility and responsiveness

Joyful Environments

Without joy, environments become toxic. Joy supports a creative and highly energized organization. Laughter lifts the spirit and encourages innovation. People who want to be at work are more productive. One need only recall the story of Ebenezer Scrooge to recognize the effect of joyful environments.

Trust Training Sessions

Training sessions to build trust must be planned and should include all team members. Many trust-building activities are available. The most popular is the Trust Walk. Team members are paired; one is blindfolded and the other is designated to lead the first on a walk. The leader has responsibility to direct the walk safely and to warn of hazards. When a person relies totally on another and the experience proves positive, trust increases. Employees who trust each other are more apt to work as a team to achieve the organization's goals. Would a quarterback throw to a receiver if he did not trust that player to catch the ball? The same is true in organizations. Team members need each other for ideas, solutions, and support. Only those they trust are tapped.

Task Sociogram (See Chapter 7)

A task sociogram is completed by having each person write down the names of all the team members. After each name, they note why that person is needed. Interaction occurs when I need someone. A task sociogram lets me know who I need as well as who needs me. A successful manager monitors this process to ensure that everyone is needed.

Mentors (See Chapter 7)

Mentors can assist team members on a regular or a periodic basis. This support is invaluable to a new member on the team. Giving that person someone to talk with and ask questions of increases productivity and supports team effort.

More Celebrations

Effective teams celebrate special occasions; for example, birthdays and births. Celebrations are vitally important in securing relationships and building interactions. These celebrations need not be large, by-invitation events. Rather, they could begin with a special announcement in the lounge when all team members are assembled or a birthday cake or a TGIF celebration. The idea is to share and build a history together!

Celebrate team successes or risks taken. This is an area often overlooked in favor of the personal events just mentioned. If your organization supports risk-taking, celebrate risk-taking!

NORMS FOR CONFLICT AND RISK-TAKING

Established norms for dealing with conflict give each member accessibility to resolving differences overtly rather than by reverting to the "mushroom syndrome" discussed in chapter 4. Norms allow conflict to be brought out in the open. In fact, if you have an established norm that states "Conflict is a positive activity," you provide an atmosphere of problem-solving and conflict management that in turn allows for organizational growth. Other norms for conflict management are found in chapters 3 and 4.

Situations That Need Attention (SITNAs)

A SITNA opens up exploration and definition of solutions. If you refer to problems as SITNAs, or "situations that need attention," the team is empowered to attend to the problem and to control the outcome rather than being dictated to by the forces causing the problem. Viewing problems as SITNAs makes problem-solving proactive rather than reactive.

A resource for problem-solving that includes fifty-four different structuring devices for problem-solving is *The Practical Decision*

Maker by Harvey, Bearley, and Corkrum (Lanham, MD: Scarecrow Press, 2001).

Inclusive Distribution Lists

Documents represent inclusion, not just information. Every memo you write should be analyzed for inclusion. Information is power and should be treated as such at all times. Ask not only "Who needs to know?" Also ask "To whom do you want to give power in your organization? Who needs to feel included?"

Regular Employee Bulletins

Employee bulletins keep everyone informed of what is going on, giving all team members a common base of information. A bulletin may describe tasks, share personal information, and announce upcoming events. It provides information on innovations or new ideas that are coming down the pike. Publish an employee bulletin regularly.

The All-Question Meeting

From time to time, a meeting may be formatted to limit team members to asking or responding to questions. Work with team members to listen to each question rather than immediately shifting the focus to what they want to say. Questions call for listening. When people listen, they think about the concepts discussed. Questioning habits ingrained in a team can improve decision-making and problem-solving.

Clearly Articulated Performance Expectations (CAPE)

Managers who provide clear and appropriate expectations communicate a healthy level of stress, which in turn provides an atmosphere focused on the organization's goals. Employees should know at all times what is expected of them.

It is best to put these expectations into writing. Verbal expectations can be misinterpreted. A CAPE may be as simple as "you will arrive at work by 8:00" or as complex as "each team member is expected to write a recap of the week's task by Friday at 3:00 and submit it to the director." It is important to have individual CAPEs for each team member as well. These may change throughout the year or be yearly expectations. Rules for CAPEs:

1. Make them clear.
2. Make them simple.
3. Make them doable.
4. Make them support the organization's goals and visions.

Timely Feedback (See Chapter 4)

Timely feedback gives employees information on their efforts expended to date. Feedback includes positive as well as negative information. It can be accomplished through formal conferences or informal discussion. Timely feedback helps employees rethink, refocus, and reorder priorities.

Management by Walking Around (MBWA) (See Chapter 7)

The interaction characteristics of trust and relationship are reinforced through MBWA. A manager who is "out there" with the team builds both. By asking questions and listening, the manager finds out informally what the team thinks. The more questions asked, the stronger the trust. The stronger the trust, the more effective the team and the higher the energy available to reach organizational goals.

Department Tours

Employee tours of other departments encourage a broader organizational perspective. How better to get the big picture, understand your teammate's situation, and acquire a common base of information than by seeing a colleague at work? As organizational problems arise, all members provide input toward solution if they have seen it in action. Often, someone from another department sees a situation more clearly or from a different and helpful viewpoint because he or she is not bogged down with preconceived notions. Moreover, team relationships are reinforced as assistance is proffered and accepted. Remember the interdependence theme: "I need you and you need me."

Encouraging Risk

Team members should be encouraged to try new ideas—and to risk failure. Without risk, there is no change, no innovation. Encouraging your team to take bounded risks, that is, risks that have a semblance of possibility and probable success, propels the team to move beyond the accepted. Of course, not every new idea or risk yields success. Establishing a culture of bounded risk prompts creativity. Establishing acceptance of failure ensures *continued* creativity. Include risk-taking in your tenets and vision statements. Develop norms for taking risks and accepting failure. Celebrate new ideas. Write up instances of risk-taking in the staff bulletin. Learn and grow from failure.

"Take a Risk" Buttons

You might hand out "take a risk" buttons. Or use a variety of messages: "I took a risk" . . . "Do you have a new idea?" Find phrases that send the message "It's okay to try out new ideas around here!"

The Next-Time Norm

A powerful organizational question is "How would you do it differently another time?" Norms are powerful. When team members establish the habit of asking themselves and their colleagues this simple question, then learning occurs and new ideas are born. A next-time norm shows that errors are accepted, reinforces trust, and supports collegial relationships.

Revisiting Norms

A single session to write and discuss norms does not institutionalize them, but norms that are revisited pervade the organization. Behaviors important enough to state are important enough to establish firmly and to reinforce within the organization. A norm about taking risks or tolerating errors fades quickly if not restated. Use staff meetings to review your agreed-upon norms. Are other norms needed? Are some not working? Why? Chapter 3 describes a process to follow when you revisit norms.

Broadcasting Change

Broadcasting changes in personnel, product, and process gives everyone a common base of information. Staff meetings, bulletins, celebrations, and memos—all are appropriate vehicles for broadcasting change.

Play and Good Works

Relationships can be built and strengthened in play and good works. Establish a fitness club, sports team, or charity focus. Initiating an athletic team or targeting a specific charity for the organization to support gives members a common purpose. It establishes their identity and willingness to work together. Functioning as a team in such projects encourages flexibility and responsiveness as members learn to react to problems and to be proactive together for a shared goal.

"Unmeetings"

You might try scheduling an "unmeeting" in which team members just talk. Grand ideas emerge when people "just talk." Questioning techniques can be reinforced, too. Informal settings engender a healthy level of stress as members, though not expected to "perform," nevertheless find implicit challenge in bouncing ideas around and off each other.

INTERDEPENDENCE ANALYSIS

To strengthen the eight characteristics of interaction, team members must need, and know that they need, each other. The Interdependence Analysis helps team members understand how each member is needed. Continually ask: "Whom do you need to accomplish this task?" and "Who needs you to accomplish his or her tasks?" If someone is never needed, the thoughtful manager asks why. And the manager knows that an individual who is needed by everyone but needs no one else holds a great deal of power. An Interdependence Analysis assesses that balance within the organization.

Interdependence Analysis

Tasks this month   Who I needed to help complete the task

1. Who isn't on the list?

2. Have I needed any of the people on List 1 in the last six months? Why? Why not?

STRUCTURE AND CONTEXT

- Clear understanding/acceptance of group structure
- Periodic attention to group maintenance
- Recognition/mitigation of outside forces

Norm-Setting Again

The potency of norm-setting is reflected in the frequency with which it comes up. To strengthen this aspect of team effectiveness, norms are set to determine group structure. Establishing how the team will operate provides a clear understanding of that structure. The next chapter is entirely devoted to this essential norm-setting process.

The "Ten-Minute Team"

Described by Thomas Isgar in 1989, this brief exercise, followed routinely at the beginning of each meeting, brings out many of the energy-sapping problems or processes that may be occurring in the organization. To implement the ten-minute team concept, spend the first ten minutes of each meeting dealing with process. Ask: "How are we doing?" . . . "Are our norms working?" People need to vent, to discover whether others share their feelings, and to be empowered to make necessary changes. The ten-minute team exercise allows this to happen.

Clear Expectations—Again

This item, too, appeared earlier in this chapter. Attending to clear expectations supports structure and context as well as interaction. Do your employees know what is expected of them? Do they understand where they fit in the organization's structure? Do not assume they fathom these matters just because they have job descriptions and organizational charts. Be clear about your expectations. Meet with each member of the team individually. Be specific about what you expect. Elicit from them questions or concerns they may have. Never make them second-guess your intentions.

THE INTERACTION METHOD OF MEETING MANAGEMENT

A useful approach for managers is to establish rotating roles of facilitator, recorder, and process observer at each meeting, as described by Doyle and Straus in *How to Make Meetings Work*. Tradition suggests that the manager or boss runs meetings, but Doyle and Straus argue for other arrangements. By rotating the roles of facilitator, recorder, and observer, all members take on each responsibility in turn.

What are these roles? A facilitator ensures that everyone is heard and that consensus is reached. A facilitator does not discuss content but keeps the meeting moving efficiently by clarifying and restating. This neutral party ensures that all members are heard. A recorder takes minutes, frequently on large chart pads to make certain that suggestions and decisions are accurately reflected. Team members are then free to discuss rather than take notes. A process observer watches *how* decisions are reached. At the end of, or periodically during, the meeting the observer reports on team behavior. Are group norms happening? Are members listening to each other? Has everyone had a chance to interject ideas? Are decisions coming by consensus or are they ramrodded through by a few? Are side conversations occurring? These are but a few of the group maintenance processes to be observed.

Set the Agenda

The agenda should be set ahead of time and reviewed for additions. Usually, the facilitator will set the agenda but it may be set by the decision-maker. Times should be specified for each item.

PITS Model

It is very important to use the PITS model (Harvey, Bearley, and Corkrum 2001):

P—Personal
I—Interpersonal
T—Task
S—Summary

In making meetings work, you must allow individuals to talk about the personal or to send interpersonal messages at the beginning of the meeting or they will intrude on the business of the meeting. They might want to talk about their child's Little League victory or their mother's illness or their trip to Mazatlan. They may want to thank a fellow worker or ask for help or phone a fellow worker for committee work. You can limit the time to five minutes or so, but allow some time for the personal and interpersonal. You then go on to the tasks of the meeting freed of personal baggage. Finally, you should end the meeting with a summary of what was agreed upon, who is responsible, and when it will be done.

Establish Decision Set

For each item on the agenda, there are four decision sets (Harvey, Bearley, and Corkrum 2001):

- Convenience: You make the decision because it doesn't make much difference, such as where to go to lunch.
- Command: You must command the decision, and time and safety are issues to consider.
- Consultation: You are going to make the decision after input from others.
- Consensus: The group is going to make the decision because it is an issue of values and trust is important.

It is time wasted to act as if an item is a consensus decision when it is really a convenience decision. To have a long, protracted discussion about where to go to lunch is costly in terms of time. In order to use a meeting efficiently, you must specify what is the appropriate decision set.

Walk Around

No one said that when you are a facilitator you have to be a sitting target. In fact you are much better off if you are moving. We recommend that as a facilitator you walk around, not frenetically, but with calm and determination.

Two-Minute Meeting

When you feel that the meeting is not going well, you may call time out. Then call on the process observer to report on how the meeting is going. You can, in this way, control the course of the meeting.

In these ways, you can control the course of the meeting and the time allotted too. You can save 30 to 50 percent of the meeting and give yourself the gift of time so you can do more important work.

DEBRIEFING

It is important to take time at the end of each meeting to debrief about action steps and persons responsible, as agreed. Be sure these steps and responsibilities have been recorded. After the meeting, the recorder distributes this information as a reminder to all members. Every team member leaves the meeting knowing what is to be done, who is doing it, when will it be accomplished, who will assist, and what resources are needed.

BRAINSTORMING

Time for team planning and brainstorming is also important. It should be planned for. This process may be formal or informal, but it is essential to provide forums in which brainstorming may occur. Brainstorming is an exercise that allows all members to participate in generating solutions or ideas. The suggestions are *not* evaluated as they are listed but rather after all ideas have been exhausted. Remember that truly creative ideas emerge only after at least fifteen minutes of brainstorming. Give the team sufficient time to reach innovation.

ENVIRONMENTAL SCAN

What do your clients, your community, think and want? An environmental scan searches out thinking about your organization by those on the outside. It looks at external forces and trends, clients, customers, and competition. Environmental scanning also looks internally to assess trends and assumptions. The environmental scanning process should become institutionalized; that is, a regular part of planning. Environmental scanning helps an organization become proactive rather than reactive as members constantly increase their awareness of conditions both internal and external.

THE STRATEGIC PLAN

Develop a strategic plan for the organization. According to John Bryson (1988), strategic planning is "a disciplined effort to produce fundamental decisions and actions that shape and guide what an organization is, what it does, and why it does it." Strategic planning helps an organization look at the long term, clarify future direction, and develop a coherent and defensible basis for decision-making. Organizations working from a strategic plan reach decisions in light of future consequences, establish sound priorities, and develop effective strategies. As a bonus, strategic planning helps team members solve major organizational problems, improve organizational performance, deal effectively with rapidly changing circumstances, strengthen expertise, and build teamwork. With the prospect of all these worthwhile results, is it not time to initiate strategic planning in your organization?

Strategic Planning

Steps in Strategic Planning:

1. Form an appropriate team
2. Establish a plan to plan
3. Gather appropriate data
   a. SWOT analysis (strengths, weaknesses, opportunities, and threats that face the organization)
   b. External expectations
   c. Internal expectations
   d. Forecasts about the future
   e. Analysis of the present
   f. Analysis of the past
   g. Competitor profile
4. Develop tenets
5. Create a strategic vision statement
6. Examine current programs
7. Develop new programs
8. Identify strategic issues and needs
9. Formulate strategies for managing issues and programs

10. Devise action plans to manage issues and programs (see Harvey, Bearley, and Corkrum 2001)
11. Perform financial projections
12. Review feasibility of strategic vision
13. Monitor progress
14. Adjust the plan as needed

Strategizing as a Team

Strategic planning and environmental scanning bring to the surface strategic issues facing the organization. Such issues may arise from external threats or opportunities or they may emerge from conflicts—or perceptions of conflict—within the organization itself. With the information acquired in the strategic planning process, teams can work together to develop strategies that best address the issues presented. When a team rather than an individual working independently develops strategies, not only are the strategies more comprehensive but the team buys into the solutions and supports their implementation. So involve your entire team in finding approaches to organizational issues and problems.

PRESCRIPTION FOR CHAPIN SCHOOL DISTRICT

Now let us return to Chapin School District as we described it earlier in this chapter. Have you been thinking about these team-building events as they might apply to this district? Glance back at table 2.3 to review their results on the survey of team characteristics. What would you advise the district to do?

Table 2.4 displays the prescription we gave Chapin School District. There is nothing magical about this prescription (you might have selected other ingredients), but it does address their needs. While the district was not an organization in trouble, neither was it healthy. Too many good employees were leaving and too many people were either in hiding or "retired in place."

The reader should also notice that the proposed remediation is heavily "talk-talk" (i.e., it is heavily dependent on talking issues out). Orga-

Table 2.4.   Team-Building Prescription (Chapin School District)

Need	Action
	August 20___
Mutual trust	Trust-building workshop, particularly focused on inter-dependence; task sociogram
Open/direct conflict	Ten minutes provided at each meeting to relate problems and conflicts; follow-ups on all conflicts; emphasis that conflict is okay; conflict norms established
Tolerance of error	Weekly discussion of surprises and resultant learnings Work with superintendent to become more accepting
Group maintenance	One member appointed as process observer for two months; periodical time for debriefing; staff trained in Doyle and Straus process
In-group/out-group problem	Superintendent works to spread out roles Spring management retreat focusing on relationships
	Repeat diagnosis in August one year later.

nizational development calls strongly for discourse and confrontation. The process of getting concerns and problems in the open and then discussing them becomes the keystone of organizational health. Structured devices and exercises help, but talking about the right variables is the keystone to enriched climates. Too many leaders, however, do not understand the right variables or characteristics or avoid addressing those they know to be present. Effective leaders understand the characteristics that demarcate effective teams, assess their presence in the organization, and then do something about the weaknesses. That is the essence of the first building block for richer organizational climates.

CHAPTER 3

Setting Norms

Effective teams and effective organizations behave in ways that support individuals and facilitate task achievement. Creating and expanding these productive behaviors is accomplished through norm-setting. Norms are behaviors that are widely accepted by the people within an organization. Norms form the keystone that enables the other building blocks to work effectively. They support and strengthen empowerment, team-building, conflict, and entrepreneurship. When norms are well established and widely known, they enable the fifth resource—energy—to expand as a positive force. Norms are the glue of an organization, keeping us moving forward together. This chapter explains norms, how they are created, and how they are used to build positive organizational climates.

NORMS AT HOME

Have you ever marveled at your neighbors, the Smiths, who seem to have everything under control? The kids get to Little League, dance lessons, or whatever activities have been chosen. The house is always clean and the yard manicured. All this on top of time-consuming careers! How do your neighbors juggle all these demands? We took a quick peek into their life and asked, "What are some practices generally accepted in your house?" They responded

- Everyone puts away his or her own belongings.
- The dishes are washed immediately after meals and by those who did not cook.
- Laundry is done regularly on designated nights.
- Homework is completed first thing after the kids come home from school.

- There is a place for everything, and everything is in its place.
- All family members share in chores.

The list could go on, but basically, every person in the Smith household knows these expectations for *behavior*. These expectations are clearly articulated and thoroughly understood by everyone in the household.

Conversely, the neighbors on the other side of the street, the Joneses, appear to live in constant disarray. They are continuously late. The children never have their homework. If homework is done in the evening, it is lost by morning. Looking into this family circle, we find a completely different set of behaviors. We notice that

- Belongings are strewn all over the house.
- Dishwashing is not designated to anyone in particular.
- Laundry piles up until something is needed.
- Homework may be completed anytime—or perhaps not at all.
- When something is needed, a mad scramble ensues until it can be found.
- They act as if chores are for chumps.

By now, you are getting the picture. *Behaviors* that do not support the completion of tasks abound in this household. The Joneses have accepted very different expectations, or *norms*, for behavior.

A *norm* is an operational principle or expectation that implicitly or explicitly governs the actions of a group of people.

NORMS IN ORGANIZATIONS

All organizations have norms. They exist in your home, your social group, service club, or workplace. Whether at home or in the workplace, norms provide focus for everyone in the organization. Norms guide the behavior of group members. The degree to which norms are known and accepted within an organization determines the degree to which time is saved and goals are achieved.

Norms define an organization's pattern of behavior. They are not simply rules about behavior of group members, they are also ideas about *patterns* of behavior. An organization is often judged by its established norms. The Japanese automobile industry is a case in point. Most Americans consider a Japanese car a good buy. The big four Japanese companies are known for their workplace norms of commitment, precision, teamwork, hard work, and attention to detail. Most Americans assume that the norms of the workers are translated into a high-quality automobile. In fact, without those norms, could the Japanese consistently produce automobiles that hold their value and live up to their reputation?

Schools too, are judged by their norms of behavior. A school that has established explicit norms reflecting concern for student self-esteem, dedication to lifelong learning, and a commitment to a high-quality program receives trust and praise from its community. Conversely, a school that operates under sloppy, implicit norms, where students and teachers are tardy without consequence, where staff largely ignore individual students' needs, and where teachers leave each day as soon as school is out, is viewed as mediocre at best.

Norms not only hold together an organization's patterns of behavior, they also become the lens through which the organization is viewed. Norms determine whether an organization will become high-performing and productive—or low-performing and nonproductive.

CHARACTERISTICS OF BEHAVIORAL NORMS

Six basic characteristics reveal the nature and function of norms (table 3.1). Remember these characteristics; they will help you create useful, operative norms and identify those that must be revisited.

Productive or Nonproductive

Why do the Smiths accomplish so much? Because the productive behaviors are well-known expectations for everyone in the family. The

Table 3.1.   Characteristics of Behavioral Norms

- Productive or nonproductive
- Approved or disapproved
- Known or unknown
- Shared or private
- Formal and explicit or informal and implicit
- Up to date or out of date

rules have been clearly outlined and are understood by all. Later in this chapter you will see how such norms are reinforced so the productive behaviors continue.

Of course, the neighbors across the street also have expectations of family members. However, those expectations result in *non*productive behaviors that do little to help the family accomplish its tasks.

Typically, nonproductive norms appear in organizations in the absence of clear norms pertaining to specific situations. The Joneses failed to define clear norms for expected behaviors. By default, rather than intention, the end result was a set of nonproductive norms that failed to facilitate task achievement. Lack of clear norms does not preclude the existence of norms. It just precludes *productive* norms!

A second source of nonproductive norms is organizational history. Norms regulate the behavior patterns of the organization's members. Often, organizations develop norms for a specific situation; later, even though that situation may no longer exist, the norm remains—a genuine anachronism.

One company we worked with had previously experienced severe financial crisis due to mismanagement of funds. The organization had developed a norm requiring that all expenditures be approved by the CEO. The company was reorganized and, after the first year, began to show a profit. The company continued to grow rapidly and expanded its services. All expenditures continued to be approved by the CEO. Within a short time, the company was losing market share and appeared to be falling back into financial crisis. Called in to assess the situation at this point, we found through observation and discussion that the problem lay in their norms. The CEO was bogging down the process by continuing to approve all expenditures. The crisis that had initially led employees to invent this procedure had passed, yet the norm was still in operation. Once the bottleneck was broken and each department head given latitude to make financial decisions, the company regained its previous market share and a second financial crisis was averted. This old, outdated, and now nonproductive norm might once again have thrown this company into financial difficulties. The moral of this story is that norms should not be allowed to continue without periodic review.

Approved or Disapproved

A norm reflects approval or disapproval of certain behaviors. For a norm to have effect, people must continue to express approval or disapproval.

In the workplace, approval and disapproval are conferred in many ways. The manager pats an employee on the back or colleagues smile or frown in response to an exhibited behavior. More serious or formal approval may take the form of a promotion, bonus, award, or other recognition. Formal disapproval, on the other hand, is expressed through suspension or dismissal.

Why do people influence others to comply with certain norms? One reason is to help the group achieve its goals. Another is to help the group maintain itself. Members of a group reinforce the norm and influence others by approving or disapproving specific behaviors.

Known or Unknown

Norms that are widely known lower anxiety within an organization. Conversely, norms create confusion and heighten anxiety for anyone not "in the know."

What happens when you go to the movies? The expectations are generally well known. You stand in a line, usually demarcated with a guide rope at larger theaters, to purchase your ticket. You join yet another line, indicated by a sign, to enter the lobby. Possibly you queue up in a third line as you wait for entrance to the theater itself.

Several years ago, while visiting Japan, we had an opportunity to attend a movie without our trusted translator, our daughter. At first we found ourselves concerned over not speaking the language and uncertain as to what was expected. Typical of his age, our junior-high-age son was the most self-conscious. Although he knew no one there, he did not want to make a fool of himself. To our collective relief, we found, upon arriving, the same waiting lines as at any movie house back home. At the movies, whether in the United States or Japan, the expected behavior is similar, making the excursion an enjoyable affair in either country. The norms are widely known.

A symphony concert, on the other hand, raises more anxiety. A concert hall is similar to a movie theater, yet many people shy away from symphony programs because they are uncertain about what is acceptable behavior. The first surge of anxiety comes if you need to pick your tickets up from "Will Call." Where is it located? Will the tickets be there? With tickets finally in hand, you enter the theater not knowing where to go. Fortunately, a patient usher leads the way, but once inside, that dreaded anxiety rush comes once again due to uncertainty about behavior. When do you applaud? How will you know it is time for an intermission? Have you ever made the unforgivable error of clapping at the wrong place in the program? Immediately hundreds of sets of eyes peer down at you—or so it feels. You have no doubt that your behavior is disapproved. In the future, knowing it may be inappropriate to clap at particular moments, you will take care to assess the clapping behavior of others before embarking on your own.

However, this level of anxiety decreases in direct proportion to the number of times a person has attended a concert. Knowing the norms reduces anxiety. Unknown expectations for behavior cause confusion, confusion causes anxiety, and anxiety diminishes productivity or enjoyment.

What about attending an unfamiliar cultural or religious event? At the symphony, at least you can relax when the music begins, therefore feeling some level of comfort. But have you ever been to an event that is totally foreign, yet you are expected to behave or participate according to the mores of that group? Do you know when to stand, sit, or kneel? Is it all right to talk? Are you expected to sing? Is it proper to leave your seat or are you expected to do so?

A couple reported to us that on a visit to an island in the Aegean Sea, they attended a Greek Orthodox service. The moment they entered, they were uncomfortable. The wife was dressed in yellow, while the other women in the church were dressed in black. The husband and wife were told to sit in separate sections—he with the men, she with the women. Right in the middle of the service, the priest motioned to the wife. She did not understand. Eventually he came down from the altar and gestured to her to uncross her legs. For women to cross their legs was improper in this church. The couple did not know what to expect or do and were nervous throughout the service.

How much more enjoyable and productive might it be if norms for behavior were known in advance, as they are for attending the movies? Consider the employees in your organization. How well are the norms for behavior known? When your employees are at work, do they feel as if they are at the movies—or at the symphony? Are unknown behavioral requirements, such as those experienced at cultural or religious events, keeping people away from new activities or projects?

Shared or Private

If a norm is to be well known, it must be shared. That is, most people must agree on the range of behavior that is acceptable. The family in the first example clearly shared the norms that operated in their household. Everyone in the company whose CEO was signing every expenditure clearly shared that norm—to the extent that it took an outsider to identify the norm as a problem. Those attending a symphony concert for the first time find the experience more difficult because the norms are not shared. They are not written in the program; therefore, the first-time concertgoer must ask friends or rely solely on observation.

If people are left to their own devices to "figure out" norms, time is lost. And energy, that precious fifth resource, is expended in directions that do not meet the goals of the organization. Employee handbooks may describe the expectations of the organization, but how often is even that content discussed? Do employee groups where you work take time to review the norms? Are the norms productive . . . or nonproductive? Are they bought into . . . or ignored?

Organizations have many norms that are not written in handbooks. Are those norms shared equally with all employees? For example, some organizations hold a company picnic on a weekend. Are all employees expected to go? Is the picnic truly optional or is attendance an unspoken requirement for all employees?

Stop to examine your organization. List the norms—the behaviors that are expected of everyone. How did you find out about these norms? Have they been shared with your colleagues?

For a manager, consciously sharing norms is as important as providing other information to employees. Effective organizations that we work with take time at staff meetings to discuss the norms that have been established. Communicating in this manner allows the expectations to be shared—and revised as needed. Members of an organization that has shared norms for behavior work toward common goal attainment in a consistent manner. They know what is expected and what is *un*acceptable. Basically, they know "how things are done around here."

Norms must be shared with new members. Have you ever been new to a group? What happens to new members of an organization? To the new person in a group or organization, the norms may be unclear and confusing, yet those same norms are sources of order among the established membership. The longer it takes an individual to understand expectations, the longer it takes to become an effectively functioning member of the organization. Conversely, new members are easily assimilated when behavioral guidelines and expectations are well known. Therefore, it is imperative that someone in the organization spend time explaining the organization's operating norms to the new member.

I remember how invaluable the time given me by the principal was when I was a new teacher. I was fresh from academia and knew only the theory of education and the principles of child development. Each week the principal met with the core of five new teachers and explained "how things are done around here." I learned that it was critical to be friendly with the custodian, to be sure all textbooks were protected with paper covers, and to ask permission before bringing animals into the classroom. In sharing these and many other norms operating at that school, the principal enabled my colleagues and me to concentrate on honing our teaching skills, free of worries about "doing the right thing." The goals of the school advanced more rapidly because, with norms openly shared, the new members were not dissipating energy in fruitless directions.

Explicit and Formal or Implicit and Informal

Explicit, or Formal, Norms

Norms shape people's overt actions, their thoughts, and their feelings. Norms, although always well-defined rules of the group, may be explicit or implicit. Explicit norms are formal expectations for behavior within an organization.

Formal, or explicit, norms exist to help an organization attain its goals. Group members learn explicit norms through written or verbal communication. Explicit norms may deal with dress, attendance, conduct of meetings, or other issues in behavior of group members. Formal norms may be communicated, for example, in staff handbooks, guidelines for meetings, classroom rules, or office procedures.

Just as the Smiths had clearly defined rules for their household, organizations need to define expectations for behavior at work. As the principal assigned to a newly established school, I took care to have the staff develop norms describing how we were to operate. Among the norms were those that addressed professional attire and behavior. The staff was enthusiastic in their implementation of these norms, which were revisited regularly at staff meetings and revised as necessary. The staff often referred to these norms as situations arose.

How well did the staff buy in to the concept of explicit norms? The following story highlights their commitment to our staff norms—as well as their sense of humor.

On a particularly hectic morning before the starting bell had rung, I was called out of a meeting to "an emergency in Room 1." I went hurrying down to the room only to find five of my newly tenured teachers dressed in bathrobes and slippers. They were lounging around drinking coffee and reading the morning newspaper. Posted up on the board was the following list of "Norms for Newly Tenured'Teachers":

1. Thou shalt not arrive at school before your students.
2. Thou shalt not be on time to staff meetings.

3. Thou shalt not perform adjunct duties with any enthusiasm.
4. Thou shalt not confront . . . just grieve it!
5. Thou shalt not meet thy goals and objectives.
6. Thou shalt not wear hose, pumps, or dress professionally.

As I took in the scene, I glimpsed smiles that soon broke into laughter at the shocked look on my face. When a pattern of behavior—in this case, recognizing explicit norms—is taken to its extreme and becomes a focus of humor, you know the norm has become internalized and institutionalized! Humor is a powerful tool for spoofing human foibles—and at the same time recognizing genuine expectations for behavior.

Whether seriously or humorously, norms must be formally stated. When we do norm-setting workshops—whether with businesses or schools or city governments—we propose that their norms be written on large posterboards and hung on the walls. This step makes the norms visible and real so everyone can see and follow them.

Implicit, or Informal, Norms

Implicit norms are informal expectations for members' behavior. These expectations are usually learned by observing the actions of other group members. Informal norms are sets of approved and disapproved behaviors that are not written down but are rather understood as "the way things happen in this organization." Informal norms are often more powerful than the explicit, formal variety.

A very dynamic and highly successful salesperson joined a graphics firm. She had a warm personality and caring attitude toward all the office workers. However, after several weeks on the job, she found that she was not receiving messages and that her orders were not processed promptly. She was stymied as to the reason. Her past history led her to believe she was treating the office personnel with the same appropriate respect that had earned her high regard in her field. What was the problem? Upon further examination, she discovered that the other salespeople consistently went into the break room to chat with the office staff. While the new salesperson was always polite and concerned about the workload of the office staff, she was unaware of this informal norm for behavior. Once she became aware of it and began stopping in at break time, her messages were quickly passed through and her orders immediately processed.

A socialization process occurs that allows new members to learn of the expectations, the values, the ways of doing things. Likewise, new members may learn the nuances or unstated rules by imitating the implicit norms modeled by others in the organization. Reinforcement by co-workers and supervisors, as described previously, indicates which of the explicit and implicit norms are the most important.

Up to Date or Out of Date

All organizations undergo change. As they do, it is vital that they review the current norms. Organizations change out-of-date to up-to-date routines and patterns by learning how to replace old norms with new ones. The addition of one new member may dramatically alter existing patterns of behavior—especially if the new member is the CEO! Taking time at staff meetings to discuss the norms for your organization will keep them current.

Periodically, I open meetings with a "What's working, what's not" session. These ten- or fifteen-minute periods allow staff members an opportunity to voice concerns over existing norms, reinforce norms that are working, and request that new norms be developed. This process allows the norms to support the goals of the organization by expanding, not expending, energy.

STEPS IN NORM-SETTING

Norms in New Groups

When a new group forms—whether social, professional, or ad hoc—members come together for a purpose. Imagine yourself in that first meeting of the group. One member voices the opinion that meetings should begin on time, even though not everyone has arrived. That member then sits back and waits expectantly for responses to her suggestion to begin. If those present are of like mind, the meeting begins. Interaction continues until a question arises: "Do we want to meet on

Tuesdays?" How will the decision be reached? By voting or by consensus? The process continues as members gingerly, and only as need arises, offer suggestions about how the group might operate. This approach is long and laborious.

How much better and more efficient for this group if members begin by setting clear norms. This new group can begin immediately to discuss how to operate before an issue begs attention. By developing their norms up front, all the members understand and agree upon the process to be used by the group. When the time comes to talk about meeting dates, the group will already have established a norm of reaching decisions through consensus. With that understood, the group can focus on the decision, not the decision-making process. Taking time at the beginning to establish norms allows the group to proceed toward its primary goals.

For most groups, you will use the steps outlined in table 3.2a. However, if a group will not be meeting very often or is an ad hoc committee with one or two tasks, it is more expedient to use the following method.

Norms in Established Groups

As described earlier, norms may be explicit or implicit and must continue to be approved if they are to continue. However, individual

Table 3.2a. Quick Steps in Norm-Setting

1. Distribute four 3x5 cards to each committee member.
2. Ask them to write one norm or expectation they have to make the meetings run smoothly.
3. Have a recorder write comments on a large piece of whiteboard that all can see. Go around the table and let each person state one norm from a card (i.e., begin and end on time).
4. After each member's statement, ask the group if they agree or have some reservations about that norm.
5. When the group reaches consensus about the norm, leave it on the whiteboard.
6. Move to the next person and repeat steps 4 and 5.
7. Continue until all cards have been read and norms established.
8. This process should take no longer than fifteen minutes.
9. Post the norms at every meeting of the group.

behaviors also receive approval or disapproval. When a behavior is repeated and continues to be approved by the group, implicit norms come into being. Many times groups allow implicit, nonproductive norms to be established by remaining silent or by failing to disapprove a behavior. Once these implicit norms become a part of a group's operating patterns, they do not go away by themselves. Typically, only a formalized process of setting or revisiting norms will eliminate nonproductive norms.

New organizations need to begin immediately to discuss "how we are going to operate and behave." Members of new organizations are fortunate in their opportunity to set the pattern for behavior at the onset. However, few organizations have that chance. In most organizations, members will be reviewing and changing existing norms. The following will assist in that endeavor.

To change existing norms, begin at Step 1. To develop norms in a new organization, begin at Step 3 (table 3.2b).

SETTING NORMS: PREVENTION VERSUS INTERVENTION

Prevention Norms

These norms are easy to develop and will guide the organization or group through rocky times with relative ease. Prevention norms are developed when a new group is forming, when a new member is added, and when a team is revisiting norms. Prevention norms are usually more general in nature and apply to how the organization behaves on a regular basis.

Table 3.2b. Steps in Norm-Setting

1. Identify the operating norms, both explicit and implicit.
2. Distinguish productive from nonproductive norms.
3. Define the norms you want as your operating principles.
4. Determine which norms must be explicit, which may be implicit.
5. Analyze the discrepancy between the real norms and the ideal norms.
6. Reach consensus on new norms.
7. Reinforce the new norms.

New Organization

When coming together in the beginning, everyone on the team is usually expectant and looking forward to a new experience. They are looking for structure for the new group. This is the time to develop the rules of behavior or norms. Just think about raising a teenager. Beginning at age thirteen with rules is a lot easier than starting them at sixteen or seventeen when your teenager knows it all and is seeking independence. The same is true for organizations. It is much more difficult to change implicit norms than reinforce explicit norms from the outset.

New Member

As you welcome a new member to the organization, it is important to review the norms. Knowing up front what expectations are accepted by all will make assimilation into the group easier. Have you ever spent the night at someone's house and have not been quite sure of the routines, such as "Should I strip the bed in the morning?" "Am I expected to help with breakfast?" "Will there be breakfast served?" "If I get up early, can I turn on the TV?" Your stay is much more comfortable when the host lists out all of his or her expectations upon arrival. The same is true with a new member to your organization. Prevention is in order.

Revisiting

Step 7 in table 3.2b speaks of reinforcing the new norms. An important step in this process is to revisit your norms when there is not an infraction of the norms. At each meeting, the team can be asked which norms are working and which are not. Discussion should follow for norms that are not working. Do they need to be changed or is the team just being negligent? As a group you can decide when there is relative quiet.

Intervention Norms

While prevention norms are easily established with clearer thinking and a calmer atmosphere, intervention norms arise from a conflict.

Intervention norms are used in toxic environments, interpersonal conflicts, boundary conflicts, and perceptual conflicts. Oftentimes norms set in these situations are not developed by consensus but rather determined by a supervisor or mediator.

Toxic Environments

Toxic environments usually take time to develop. A new supervisor is hired who does not care about the current culture and ignores it. Issues fester, but people won't bring up their dissatisfaction until it is too late to apply a simple fix. Or it could be that bad behavior has been allowed to continue for a long time. Key members of the team are always late but are never admonished by supervisors. Employees are allowed to complete minimal work or low expectations are enforced by administration. Soon everyone becomes dissatisfied and the lunchroom and parking-lot discussions take place. Sides get drawn up. People do not want to go to work and leave as soon as they can each day. This is a toxic environment that needs norm-setting immediately!

Interpersonal Conflicts

Sometimes a supervisor must call in two employees who must work together but do not get along. This situation happens in every workplace at one time or another. In one of my offices, I inherited an interpersonal conflict between two employees. I had to set up norms immediately. They were simple in nature, and over the years, the behaviors required by the norms actually changed their attitudes toward one another. One norm was that they would greet each other in the morning and upon leaving work each day. Another norm stated that they could only say good things about one another to a third party. Interpersonal conflict norms should be few in number and simple to enforce.

Boundary Conflicts

Whether it is caused by boundary penetration or boundary expansion, these conflicts need norm-setting. Boundary penetration occurs when someone tries to take on another's job or task. Boundary expansion occurs when you try to give someone more to do than that person thinks is his or her responsibility. When site-based management first hit education, many principals felt that the teachers wanted their job, that they wanted to make decisions about how to spend money or what to purchase. Their domain was being penetrated and they didn't appreciate it. Over the years, norms developed about what to expect and how schools would be run under the new system, but it did take years. Had the staff developed new norms at the time, it would have been clear to everyone involved how the school was to function.

Boundary expansion happens in every workplace in the twenty-first century. As the workforce is pared back, new jobs, tasks, and roles are divided up among those who are left—whether they want them or not! Conflicts arise when people are frustrated about not having a say and feel unable to complete all the work. How much better it would be if norms such as "It is expected that you will dialogue with your supervisor when feeling overloaded" or "Even with more work, everyone needs a break time and should take it" were overtly stated. When they hear these statements, the workers do not feel that they have been left to their own devices to manage more work in the same amount of time. They feel that they are part of a team and that the team will achieve its goals together.

Perceptual Conflicts

You think one thing and I think another, but faced with data or information we can each see things the same. It's getting to that point that is difficult. Norms such as "We will examine all pertinent data before proceeding" or "We will have an open mind and ask questions" are helpful in perceptual conflicts. They are the easiest of the intervention norms to set and should be used whenever this conflict arises.

Proceeding Step by Step

Step 1. Identifying the Operating Norms, Both Explicit and Implicit

The group should begin by brainstorming about the norms that are currently operating. The next step is to decide whether each norm listed

---

Norm-Setting in Conflictual Situations

- Works best with interpersonal conflict
- Works best with boundary conflicts
- Works best with perceptual conflicts
- Requires more direction from supervisors
- Defines expected behavior
- Shifts focus from the "what" to the "how"
- Is versatile and immediate

---

is explicitly stated or just implicitly observed. Quite a discussion may ensue at this point, as some members will have experienced a conscious sharing of norms by others in the organization, thus insisting that the norms are explicit. Other group members, on the other hand, will have observed the behavior and accepted it as "the way things are done around here."

A case in point is a group of doctoral students who were told very explicitly by one professor in an informal setting that all assignments should be fastened with two staples in the corner, not bound. Other students, although never told directly, observed the manner in which papers were submitted. "Two staples in the corner" soon became an implicit norm for that institution. The question was never asked, however, about what the other professors preferred. When another professor casually mentioned to a group of students that he appreciated assignments that were spiral-bound, the students were confused. As it turned out, when the norm was finally discussed with all the students and professors in attendance, the explicit norm for the doctoral students became "Follow your personal preference." Much organizational energy and "grapevine" conversation was squandered on this relatively trivial case until it was confronted directly and explicitly. Do not assume that trivial issues consume trivial resources!

Step 2. Distinguish Productive from Nonproductive Norms

Using the list that results from the brainstorming session, identify which norms are productive for the organization and which are nonproductive. For example, an organization that has established a norm for tardiness would identify it as nonproductive. After reviewing all the norms in this manner, group members would determine which of the nonproductive norms should be changed. This step gives members a concrete way of dealing with behaviors that prevent the group from reaching its goals.

Step 3. Define the Norms You Want as Your Operating Principles

This can be your wish list! Now is the time to develop norms that would be ideal for the organization. If the group has never had a regular meeting day and time, here is an opportunity to suggest they be established. If your organization has downsized with the norm of attempting to do all the tasks that had been performed by a larger staff, this is the time to suggest appropriate operating procedures for discussing and resolving those issues. Public-sector and private-sector organizations alike are finding that financial, political, and social changes are driving them to review their operations to meet all the demands placed upon them. New operating norms may facilitate the process.

Step 4. Determine Which Norms Must Be Explicit, Which May Be Implicit

Some implicit norms are best brought to the surface and made explicit. Often, implicit norms are more powerful than existing explicit norms. However, by bringing an implicit norm to the surface, discussing the reasons it exists, and making it formal and explicit, you add an accountability factor. Once the members of your organization have openly stated that they agree to a norm, they become responsible for the expected behavior.

Implicit norms are not always desirable, however. Just like undesirable behavior in a classroom, undesirable but informal norms are sometimes best left alone, sometimes best confronted, and sometimes best approached indirectly. Ask yourself whether the norm negatively impacts the needs of the organization. If not, it is best left alone to flourish or die on its own.

Should you decide that a norm is truly undesirable, consider how many people will see things your way if the norm is brought to the surface and discussed. If the norm is diverting energy from goal attainment but engenders a strong emotional commitment from a majority of the people in the organization, the direct approach may not be best. In this situation, one might look for a "good habit" that will be inconsistent with the nonproductive norm, engender widespread support, and eventually replace the undesirable pattern. This decision takes you away from uncovering implicit norms and into the process of announcing and establishing an entirely new behavioral norm.

In working with the staff of a new school, determining whether a particular norm should be explicit became extremely important. Many of the members wanted to establish a formally stated, explicit norm that would require staff to dress professionally at all times. Others felt it was unnecessary to make such a statement explicit in the list of norms; they felt that the norm could be accepted as "the way we do things around here." After much discussion, the staff came to consensus that the norm would be explicit but not written down.

This step in the process becomes critical. If every norm must be explicitly stated in writing, the employee handbook becomes unmanageable. Organizations should select only the most important operating principles to state in writing. Other expectations can be shared verbally and discussed periodically.

Step 5. Analyze the Discrepancy between the Real Norms and the Ideal

Compare the items on the brainstorming list with the ideal list. Does the group see nonproductive norms that need changing? If so, participants should highlight, then prioritize, the nonproductive norms.

Before embarking on a course to change existing norms, ask the following questions:

- Which norms help the organization achieve its purpose?
- Which norms were developed under different circumstances that no longer exist?
- Which norms are harmful?

- Which norms inhibit the organization's success?
- Which norms are compatible with the goals and values of the organization? Which are not?
- Do certain norms exist because of particular conditions?
- How can the norms best be reconsidered or changed to permit the group to achieve its purposes while simultaneously *maximizing* resources?

Step 6. Reach Consensus on New Norms

Remember that "norm" is defined as "a behavior that is widely accepted by the people within the organization." The key phrase here is "*widely* accepted." The process of consensus allows someone to *disagree with the norm* but still *agree to support it*. (For more on the process of consensus, read *How to Make Meetings Work*, by Michael Doyle and David Straus.)

Step 7. Reinforce the New Norms

The process of developing or changing norms will be to no avail unless the new expectations are carefully monitored and reinforced. Consistent approval is critical to establishing the new behavior. Without reinforcement, members of an organization slip back into the old patterns and operate under nonproductive norms. If the group establishes a new norm stating that all meetings commence on time but the leader delays beginning until everyone is present, the explicitly stated norm will die. It will be replaced by an implicit norm that says "We wait until everyone is present before beginning a meeting." Being tardy will become the norm. Often, once the norm about tardiness is in place, members arrive later and later. If, however, the leader begins every meeting exactly on time, members soon learn to change their behavior and arrive promptly. New norms will persist only if reinforced.

Revisit Your Norms

Setting norms and reinforcing them are critical to the success of your team's behavior. However, oftentimes we forget to go back and look at a norm to see why it was there in the first place. We have all heard the story of the woman who always cut the end off of her whole ham prior to cooking it and was showing her children how to do it when grandma walked in and asked her what she was doing. "Well, I'm showing the children how to cook a ham, just the way you used to." Grandma responds, "You silly, I only cut the end off because I didn't have a big enough pan!" Sometimes that happens to our workplace norms. The president of a company must sign everything because that is how it was when the company was small and only had ten employees. Now that there are 100 employees, the president's norm of signing everything is actually a bottleneck to efficiency. Revisiting norms is important in order to keep them productive and up to date.

PROCESS ISSUES IN SETTING NORMS

As your organization develops and recognizes existing norms, there are some process issues for you to consider. The guidelines in table 3.3 will assist in norm-setting.

Include All Members of the Group

Norms, both formal and informal, become entrenched in organizations very quickly. They become "the way we do things around here" in a matter of weeks, if not sooner, where they are known and commonly agreed upon. Therefore, to change an existing norm, *everyone* involved must participate and collaborate in setting new norms. Only through broad collaborative participation will a new norm replace what exists.

Table 3.3.   Process Issues in Setting Norms

- Include all members of the group.
- Be sure the leader supports the change.
- Involve members in identifying the norm(s) to be changed.
- Allow members to communicate feelings and frustrations.
- Identify reasons for concern over existing norms.

Be Sure the Leader Supports the Change

A norm that is not supported by the leader becomes nonproductive. Suppose the existing norm allows employees to take a thirty-minute lunch, but they all agree to increase that time to thirty-five minutes. Without the leader's support, conflict will inevitably arise. Such conflict drains the energy of the organization from achieving its goals.

The leader's lack of support may be more subtle, even unintentional. Consider the leader who has become convinced that shared decision-making will yield higher productivity and a more humane work setting. Then suppose that the first time (and second and third) that a recommendation is generated from the new process, the leader—perhaps from force of habit, perhaps due to lack of time, perhaps through failure to see the inconsistency—summarily dismisses the idea. Overt, formal commitment notwithstanding, shared decision-making will not become operative in that organization. The leader's support must be genuine and consistent if a new norm is to flourish.

Involve Members in Identifying the Norm(s) to Be Changed

A new CEO may realize that employees are arriving late to work on a regular basis. Further inquiry reveals that this norm has existed for many years. The probability that the CEO will change the behavior simply by issuing a decree is minuscule. The employees may comply at first, but they will not be happy. In the end, unless strict sanctions are imposed, they will fall back into their old pattern.

Rather than issuing an ultimatum, draw employees into a discussion of the existence of the norm and possible remedies. In this way, ownership for the new norm shifts to the employees themselves. The new CEO becomes not a policeman but the empowering leader who has involved the staff in important decisions.

Allow Members to Communicate Feelings and Frustrations

The need to change a norm typically follows a change in personnel or circumstances within the organization. Often those changes will already have given rise to concerns and frustrations. Consequently, those whose behavior is affected by the norm need an opportunity to verbalize their feelings and frustrations toward the existing expectations and toward any new proposals generated by the group. Without this opportunity, not everyone will feel heard or understood. Some will be unable to move past emotional barriers to the issues. As a consequence, the old norm may remain operative in the organization even though a new one is explicitly adopted. Continuation of the old norm side by side with the new one becomes counterproductive. Only if employees feel rewarded by the new pattern will the new norm become reality.

Identify Reasons for Concern Over Existing Norms

This guideline is closely tied with the one above, but it moves beyond emotions to a more rational, more objective stage of discussion. To recognize a current concern is an important step. But ask these questions before proceeding: Does this norm negatively impact the needs of the organization? Is it widely accepted? Without *reason* to change a norm, leave it alone.

A Caution:

In defining and reviewing norms, the focus should be on how we want to behave *in the future*. While we may explore past behaviors, we do so only to define how we want to act henceforth. Too often, employees, filled with years of frustration or indifference, will turn norm-setting into an arena for blame and recrimination. This must be avoided. Nothing can be done to change the past. One can only make changes for the future. *Focus on what the group wants to become*, not how and why it got to where it is!

Group norms are basic, simple statements that tend to preserve the status quo in an organization. Typically, these norms were highly appropriate for the circumstances in which they were established; however, they may last long after they have served their purpose. For an organization to remain vital, its norms must be reviewed and reassessed regularly.

ASSESSING EXISTING NORMS

One way to assess the norms existing in your organization is to complete the Behavioral Norms Index (table 3.4). Thinking about the

Table 3.4.   Behavioral Norms Index

Norms are a group's shared expectations about behavior. They may be explicitly stated as rules or guidelines for behavior or implicitly understood as the way things happen in an organization.

Answer the following questions relative to the behaviors accepted by your employees as "the way things happen around here."

To what degree does each of the listed norms operate in your organization? Please answer according to the following scale:

1 = Not at all   3 = To some degree
2 = To a slight degree   4 = To a great degree

Decision-Making

1. Employees make suggestions about solutions to problems facing the organization.
2. Employees have responsibility for expenditures pertaining to their departments.
3. Employees are involved in important decisions in this organization.
4. Employees suggest agenda items for meetings.
5. Employees work individually to solve problems.
6. Client input is used in the decision-making process.
7. Employees support unwanted decisions.
8. Employees know the established procedures for decision-making.
9. Solutions to problems that affect the organization are determined primarily by employee groups.

Total

Risk-Taking

1. Employees try out new ideas.
2. Employees suggest new ideas or approaches without fear of reprisal.
3. The staff accepts innovation.
4. Staff members trust each other.
5. It is acceptable for innovations not to be successful.
6. Staff members receive praise or recognition for trying new ideas.
7. It's okay for people to say "I need help."
8. Employees are not heard saying "Here we go again!" when a new approach is suggested.
9. Mistakes or failures are viewed as opportunities to learn.

Total

Communication

1. Employees listen to suggestions made by others.
2. Problem-solving sessions are a regular part of employee meetings.
3. An open exchange of ideas is encouraged.
4. Employees informally discuss how they can help make things better.
5. Employees plan tasks together.
6. Employees request special meetings for problem-solving.
7. There are few side conversations at meetings.
8. All members have equal input during meetings.
9. Information regarding what is happening in the organization is shared equitably with all employees.

Table 3.4. Continued

10. People are encouraged to share their own work or tasks with others.
11. Employees include management in informal problem-solving.
12. Employees encourage client suggestions for changes in the organization.
Total

Conflict

1. Employees confront each other when conflict arises.
2. Employees who disagree with a decision support it after the decision is made.
3. Staff cliques do not exist.
4. Employees support decisions made by the group, even when they feel another decision would be better.
5. Conflicts among employees are viewed by staff as "information that does not go outside this room."
6. Conflict exists and is discussed.
7. Employees confront those who do not "pull their own weight."
8. Conflict resolution is seen as a positive activity.
9. Employees do not complain about changes occurring in the organization.
Total

Scoring and Interpretation

1. After determining the totals for each of the four areas of the Index, copy them on the lines provided. Divide each total by the number of norms listed.

Decision-making	÷ 9 =	
Risk-taking	÷ 9 =	
Communication	÷ 12 =	
Conflict	÷ 9 =	

2. Plot your Organizational Index scores below, measuring from 4, where the axes cross. You may wish to draw lines connecting the four dots.

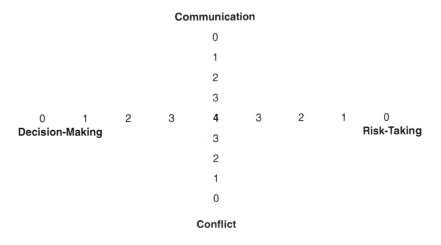

Table 3.4.   Continued

---

3. The closer to the middle your four scores fall, the stronger those norms in your organization. The farther they are out in the circumplex, the greater the problems.
4. In addition to looking at the circumplex, individual items should be examined for possible change. The lower the score on any one item, the greater the likelihood it should be addressed. Keep in mind that not all organizations need the *same* norms, but all organizations need *some* norms.

---

behaviors that currently prevail will provide a basis for selecting or revising new ones.

ADDITIONAL NORMS

The Behavioral Norms Index provides you with thirty-nine possible norms for an organization. Table 3.5 presents additional norms that may prove helpful. These are samples of norms found in various organizations. The list could be endless and is provided only as a starting

Table 3.5.   Sample Norms

Norms about Meetings

1. Meetings will begin and end on time. Employees will be on time for meetings.
2. People will pay attention to the person speaking.
3. There will be a chairperson at all meetings.
4. Members will speak only when called on.

Norms about Responsibility

1. Responsibilities will be shared equally.
2. We expect the personal best from every individual.
3. Providing assistance to colleagues is everyone's responsibility.

Norms about Standards

1. Professional attire will be worn at all times.
2. Employees are to display certifications.
3. Positive attitudes will be shown to a client at all times.
4. Diversity is exciting.

Norms about Innovation and Change

1. Change indicates growth and vitality.
2. Everything can be improved in some way.
3. Innovations need not be successful every time.

---

point. Consult *Organizational Universe Survey System* by Jones and Bearley (Organizational Design and Development, 1986), for additional examples. Together with your employees, you can reach consensus on the norms appropriate to your organization. As you work through identifying the existing and ideal norms for your organization, you will find that your own brainstormed list will give you much to work with.

CONCLUDING NOTE

Establishing clear norms for your organization can result in lower anxiety and therefore allow employees to expend and expand energy toward meeting the goals of the organization. Norms can assist you in moving your organization farther away from organizational toxicity and closer to organizational expansion, which in turn encourages team-building and intrapreneurship.

CHAPTER 4

Managing Conflict

A natural by-product of increased societal and organizational complexity has been the rise of organizational conflict. When managers are polled about their greatest people needs, they consistently point to organizational conflict as their primary managerial plague—and they are right. Effective conflict management is a critical building block for effective teams.

This building block, however, is very different from the two discussed previously. For while team-building and norm-setting were fundamentally proactive, calling on managers to craft an effective organizational climate, conflict management is reactive. Conflict occurs spontaneously, and a manager must know how to deal with it. Yes, effective managerial behavior can sometimes prevent conflict, but not always. The effective team leader must be able to respond to that conflict and control it. And sometimes controlling it seems simply impossible.

I remember a small rural school district in California that asked me to help them with team-building. A new board member had been elected (I will call him Mark) who hated the other board members. In fact, he had run on an anti-board slate. In the same election, the current board president had also been reelected, and by an overwhelming margin. Mark began visiting schools to find out what was going on and to line up his supporters. At board meetings he questioned every policy and every expenditure. He never passed up an occasion to attack the majority. Board meetings became increasingly strident, and staff picked sides or simply hid and hoped to go unnoticed. This was as toxic an organization as you can find. Finally one night the quietest board member stood up, pulled out his revolver, slammed it on the table before him and yelled, "I'm tired of your bull—, Fat Boy!" At that point the superintendent decided he could ignore the conflict no longer.

No leader can empower people, build teams, or produce positive out-comes in so toxic a setting. Conflict, which is endemic, indeed rife, in most organizations, must be managed or the organization becomes toxic. One of the tragedies in the school district situation just described was that the leader waited so long to act. He saw conflict as purely negative and hoped it would go away of its own accord. It does not—and it did not.

ROLE OF CONFLICT

Let us carry this premise even further. Not only should managers *not* be put off by the negative connotations of conflict. Rather, they should accept conflict as a necessary and productive element in organizational growth. As noted earlier, institutions and individuals that lack stress also fail to progress. While it may not feel good, conflict provides rich opportunities for organizations to grow. One of the assumptions that undergirds this premise about conflict is that human beings are prob-lem-seeking animals who need conflict to survive. What happens to someone who retires and goes home to watch television all day? The likelihood is that he will die sooner than his more active colleagues. Human beings need challenges—and that means problems—to enrich their lives.

Think of your own situation. We guarantee that if you could bring your organization to the point where it had no problems, no hassles, no dilemmas—a completely smooth operation—you would mess it up. You would try to improve the quality of customer support or add another product line or expand service areas or the like. You, too, need challenges to survive. Many of the business owners we work with sell out their businesses once they are established because they no longer find challenge when the operation requires only maintenance manage-ment. They are entrepreneurs who thirst for challenge. All of us thirst for challenge, whether we are golfers or quiltmakers or pilots or lovers or parents—or managers. Problems are the spice that enriches our lives. While most of us do not need to seek out problems—somehow they find us—the reality is that we *need* those problems and conflicts. They foster and enrich the person we are becoming.

Growth, however, does not occur naturally. It must be managed. When your child comes home from school after having had a fight, you know that is a teachable moment, a time when you can talk with him or her about what happened and what should be done. When such a moment is simply experienced, and not analyzed or reflected upon, it typically yields fear or anger, not growth. So, too, organizational conflict. It must be reflected upon and managed. We propose as an example a scenario we experienced (see below). How would you manage this conflict so as both to settle the immediate problem and to enrich the organization for the long run?

CONFLICT PRINCIPLES

There are a number of principles that you must keep in mind to handle conflict, to build a cohesive team.

You Control Conflict through Questions

We have a little experiment we want you to try. Have someone yell at you. Then ask him or her a question such as "What do you mean by that?" Immediately that person's eyes will look upward; he or she will think and then respond—but with a lowered tone. Keep asking questions and you will lower the tone even more. You've moved that person from the visceral to the cognitive domain. You've moved him or her from the stomach to the head. When you've done so, you've gone a long way toward resolving the conflict. So when conflict starts, have some ready questions in mind. "Why?" "How could I have done better?" "What do you want me to do different?" and the like. Now these can't be sarcastic questions, such as "So what?" or "Oh yeah?" They must be real questions. The true use of questions is a fine first strategy in resolving conflict.

Find Common Ground

It is important to work for the points of agreement between you—the common ground that you both share. By emphasizing what you share, you'll begin to understand how much you hold in common. By emphasizing how you differ, you'll really reverse the conflict and tear apart the team.

Use an Analytical System

By using an analytical system to master conflict, you move from your emotions to your head. You make the whole process more rational and, hence, controllable. In this way you allow the feelings to play a distant second to the conflict. One we recommend is, of course, contained in this chapter.

Forget About Winning

Winning or losing doesn't matter. They deal in the emotional states of nature. Now interests—that's another matter. What are your interests—or needs—in the conflict? They are worth fighting for, because they represent true needs. Never back off from your interests for the sake of peace. "Winning" deals with the visceral, with interest, with the substance of the conflict (Fisher and Ury 1991).

Save Face

Would you rather have a person walk away from a conflict humiliated and vowing to get even, or feeling heard and treated fairly even if he or she didn't agree with the outcome? The latter, of course. You should hear someone out and seek to save face for that person. He or she needs to leave with dignity intact. While this principle has been identified with Asian culture, it is equally true of all cultures. Save their face and they'll save yours.

Mutual Motivation for Resolutions

It seems obvious that both parties have a motivation to resolve conflict. They may have different solutions but shared motives for resolution of the disagreement—or do they? There are those among us who thrive on conflict. No matter how they try to resolve the conflict, they deflect the strategy and strive to keep the conflict going. On the surface they appear to be filled with angst but really they enjoy the conflict. Normal strategies don't work with these people. You must use strategies for difficult people. You must avoid guilt and go broken record. You must use different tactics. By observing these principles, you will be able to manage conflict more effectively. You'll never get 100 percent success, but maybe you'll get success 80 or 90 percent of the time. If that's doing better than you are doing right now, why not give it a try?

What would you do? To find the most effective answer to this question, you need to understand:

1. The conflict pollutants in organizations
2. The five types of conflict
3. The thirteen conflict resolution strategies
4. The relationship between types of conflict and resolution strategies

After we have discussed each of these topics, we will describe and analyze how we handled the following scenario. So right now, *before* you read the next paragraphs, jot down your plan of action. Then you will be able to compare your strategies with ours.

CONFLICT POLLUTANTS IN ORGANIZATIONS

Conflict pollutants are those factors that clog and choke the climate for effective conflict management. They are elements that are not inherent in the conflict itself but that distract from and complicate the resolution process. These pollutants need to be understood and cleaned out of the situation; otherwise, the conflict will be too toxic to resolve. Marc Roberts offers a particularly good description of these factors in his book *Managing Conflict from the Inside Out* (1982). Table 4.1 lists the nine conflict pollutants that we find most prevalent in group and organizational settings.

Preferences above Principles

Upon occasion, I cook dinner for our family. While I am engaged in this process, my spouse comes up to me and comments, "Why don't

Scenario: Whose Side Are You On?

Principal Michael Gárcia was not looking forward to this special meeting of the Dwight Eisenhower High School Boosters Club. When club
secretary Mary Hart called him about the meeting, she had made it clear
that her main purpose was to make sure that new lights would be in
place on the football field in time for the first home game in September.

Mike had been in the middle of the football-light controversy for
nearly a year now. Ever since the structural engineer hired by the district
had announced that the existing light standards were unsafe—that they
had deteriorated over the years to such an extent that a sudden burst of
wind, even in the 20 to 40 mph range, could topple one or more of the
standards without warning—the issue had become a high priority.
Immediately upon receiving the engineer's report, Superintendent Mar-
ian Murray had recommended to the Board of Education that further
use of the field be halted until the condemned light standards could be
removed.

Mike felt fortunate that when the board accepted the superintendent's
recommendation, only one more home football game remained for the
season. He had been successful in having that last game relocated to
their opponent's field. The unsafe light standards were subsequently
removed and the football/soccer field was again available for play—but,
of course, only during daylight hours.

Then the board decided not to include replacement of the field lights
in the maintenance budget for the year. In announcing this decision,
board president Eric Wilson stated, "The Board has been entrusted by
the community to provide for the safety and welfare of all students
throughout the district. It is unfortunate that with the tight fiscal
restraints we face today, not all of the deserving projects can be funded
next year. We are particularly unhappy that the replacement lights for
the high school football field could not be included in the budget. However, after much discussion and careful consideration, the board has
decided to include only those maintenance items that directly affect the
safety of young people throughout the district. The cost of these safety
items, in fact, exceeds the funds available for the maintenance category
next year."

Immediately upon hearing the board's action, Jim Sykes, the high
school booster club's president, leaned toward Mike and loudly whis-

pered, "We can't let them get away with this! I'm calling a special meeting of the booster club for Thursday night!"

The Thursday night special meeting turned out to be the first in a series of highly charged, emotional meetings in which the word "recall" was uttered frequently. Plans to alert the community through letters to the editor and to organize the parents of all students participating in interscholastic sports were proposed. Mike Garcia attended each of the meetings. He did his best to explain the fiscal problems facing the district and to help channel the negative energy being generated by the group toward more positive goals. The booster club had a long history of complaints and negative outlook. Mike did succeed in persuading the booster club to organize several fund-raising potluck dinners and candy sales toward the replacement of the lights. He hoped that these activities would siphon off the energy of the malcontents.

Despite the fund-raising activities, however, the monies raised had fallen far short of the amount needed, and attempts to pressure the board seemed to result in a hardening of positions on both sides. Time was running out. If the contract for new lights were not awarded soon, no night games could be played in the fall.

Mike Garcia had high regard for Superintendent Murray and appreciated the fact that the superintendent had involved him fully in preparing recommendations for the year's budget. In the budget preparation meetings, Mike, like each of the district administrators, had full opportunity to advocate for those items that he considered high priority. Mike had argued rather forcefully for inclusion of the new lights. He pointed out that without night games, most of the adult spectators in the community could not attend. Without the ticket revenues from these adult fans, money for maintenance and replacement of equipment for all interscholastic sports would fall short, thereby placing the entire athletic program in jeopardy. Of course, Mike's fellow administrators had their own needs and priorities and, in Mike's opinion, many of these were well justified on the grounds that they were addressing safety hazards. Mike had had his turn at bat and now that the recommendations had been made, he knew that the superintendent expected him to give full support to the board's decision.

As he entered the booster club's meeting room, Principal Mike Garcia could sense that something big was about to happen. All eyes turned to him as Jim Sykes exclaimed, "Good to see you, Mike. Now we can

get down to business. Well, ladies and gentlemen, we have done everything possible to get the board to change its mind about the new lights.
It's their job to get the money we need, and they haven't done it. They
have rejected the needs of the majority of students at Eisenhower High,
and I think it is now time to organize a recall campaign!"

He paused; then turned to Mike. "Well, Mike, are you with us?" he
asked.

Mike began to explain that the board was faced with many tough
decisions and that, after thorough discussion of all the district's needs,
he had to acknowledge that some of the necessary items could not possibly be approved. Before he had finished his thought, however, Jim interrupted with, "Mike, it simply comes down to this. Are you going to
support the kids in your school, or are you going to fall in line behind
the board?"

you put that pan on the front burner?" or "You ought to use this knife;
it works better," or "You'd have more space if you cleaned up after
each preparation," or the like. My spouse is trying to be helpful, but
comments like that upset me enough that I don't want to cook at all.
You see, there are certain preferences about food preparation that work
for my spouse, and that is the way I am expected to do it. Trying to
impose those preferences creates a conflict that is neither necessary nor
productive. A battle over preferences is a useless battle because it is
simply a contest over style, over choice of a way to proceed. Preferences are options, none of which are imperative.

Now principles—*those* are worth fighting over! To my spouse, balanced meals from all food groups is important, and turning the sauce-
pan handle away from the outside of the stove to prevent a small child

Table 4.1. Conflict Pollutants

1. Putting preferences above principles	6. Mushroom syndrome
2. Expecting too much	7. Poor problem ownership
3. Poor feedback skills	8. Solving before listening
4. Negativism and joylessness	9. "Last tags" complex
5. Conflict traps	

from grabbing it and pouring hot contents on himself is equally important. These are principles of cooking. They are truths; disregarding them has important consequences.

Too often organizational conflicts arise over preferences, not principles, of management.

For example:

- A school principal wants classroom bulletin boards arranged in a particular fashion.
- A city manager demands a certain orthodoxy in staff reports.
- A shop supervisor pushes for cleaner workstations at the end of the day.
- A head nurse wants medications distributed in a specific manner.
- A bank branch manager wants money counted in a certain way.
- A school board always finishes its agenda by 9:30 P.M.

These are all preferences. They work well for given individuals. The trouble occurs when your preferences differ from those of others and you assume your way is the *only* way. Each of the six situations above is a real example that led to major organizational battles. These battles did not prove productive; they simply polluted the climate. Disputes over preferences seldom achieve the goals of the organization; they are simply skirmishes about style. Be sure that when you go to war, you battle for important principles. Those are worth fighting for!

Expecting Too Much

A second pollutant is overblown expectations. "We can turn the face of this company around by next Tuesday." No, major turnarounds do not occur quickly. Change takes time, so when we expect too much too quickly, we simply create a climate for failure. People who experience failure, or anticipate that they will, get into far more conflicts than anyone else.

Think of the child who misbehaves constantly. We expect him to stop being a problem and be consistently good all the time. The very first time the kid gets into trouble, we become angry and shout: "I thought we made it clear. You are not to do that any more. Don't you understand? How many times do I have to tell you!?" The youngster then acts quite predictably. He becomes angry and frustrated and gives up trying to be good. When you expect too much, you get very little.

Change takes baby steps. Forget that truism and you engender frustration and failure. In such an environment you see defensive behavior and continual attempts to get even. The result is a quagmire of conflicts. These subsequent conflicts, however, are not really about the immediate situation; rather, they materialize out of the progenitor climate. I am mad at you not about this matter, but about an issue embedded deep inside of me—about your unrealistic expectations.

These undue expectations are not always extrapersonal. We also do this to ourselves. As of this writing, I have a graduate student who expects that every paper she writes should be superb. For the most part she is correct, but last semester I gave her a well-deserved "C." Since then she has been dejected and has engaged in fights with her close friends and colleagues and with other members of the faculty. These fights are not about the surface issue of the moment; they arise from her sense of shortfall, of not achieving what she expected. Organizations and individuals that expect too much of themselves create a climate in which unproductive conflicts flourish. In change theory, we talk of "small wins" (Harvey 1990). It is important to allow people to change in small increments. One learns to walk by taking baby steps.

Poor Feedback Skills

"You're a lousy father!" "You're a lazy bum!" "You're an ingrate!" "You're a terrible teacher!" What do I do with these statements? There is nothing I can do but get angry. I can change behavior, but I cannot change what or who I am. There are myriads of things each of us does badly, and at some point we need to know about them. But we need to find out about them in a way that allows us to change. The way I deliver a message should not cloud the content of that message. Effective feedback skills enable people to hear what you have to say and to do something about it. Table 4.2 lists a few prescriptions for effective feedback. Their overall effect will be to make you more successful at communicating your message and less likely to generate conflict.

Let us look at a few examples:

Poor: "You're a lousy worker. You don't care about your work."
Better: "For the last month your work has shown a high percentage of errors. Tell me what you think is happening."

or

Poor: "You don't love me any more. You never bring me flowers."
Better: "I'm angry. When we were first married you often told me you loved me and often brought me gifts. In the last two years, you have seldom said you love me or brought me gifts. This hurts."

or

Poor: "This is a bad paper, and you're a bad writer. But this has been true of you for years."
Better: "This paper has a number of problems. Four particular items are: (1) inconsistent use of the style manual, (2) many punctuation errors, (3) repeated lapses in paragraph connections and segues, and (4) no clear ending. The content is good, so if you attend to these problems, you will have a good paper."

How would you respond to the first criticism in each pair? Some of the most important data we can receive from (or give to) others consists of feedback related to our (or their) behavior. If we use the reactions of others as a mirror in which to observe the consequences of our own behavior, we can turn feedback into opportunities for learning. Personal data, in the form of feedback, help us become more aware of what we do and how we do it, thus enabling us to modify our behavior so we are more effective in interacting with others.

To develop and use the techniques of feedback for personal growth, it is necessary to understand certain characteristics of the process. Following is a brief set of guidelines that may assist you to do better as both a giver and a receiver of feedback. This list, displayed in table 4.2, is only a starting point. You may wish to add additional items from your own experience.

Table 4.2.   Hints for Giving and Receiving Feedback

1. Focus on behavior rather than the person.
2. Focus on observations rather than inferences.
3. Focus on description rather than judgment.
4. Focus on "more or less" rather than "either or."
5. Focus on "here and now" rather than "there and then."
6. Focus on alternatives rather than answers.
7. Focus on value to the receiver rather than satisfaction for the giver.
8. Focus on the amount of information the receiver can use rather than the amount the giver might like to impart.
9. Be sensitive to time and place.
10. As a receiver, focus on what is said rather than why it is said.

Behavior, Not Person

The first guideline is to focus feedback on behavior rather than on the person. It is important to refer to what a person does rather than to comment on what we imagine the person is. This focus on behavior further indicates use of verbs and adverbs (which relate to actions) rather than adjectives or nouns (which relate to qualities) when giving feedback. Thus, we might say someone "talked considerably in this meeting" rather than that the person "is a loudmouth." When we talk in terms of "personality traits," rather than behavior, we imply inherited, constant qualities that are difficult, if not impossible, to change. Focusing on behavior implies that it is related to a specific situation and might be changed. A person will feel less threatened to hear comments about his or her behavior rather than comments about "traits."

Observations, Not Inferences

Effective feedback focuses on observations. Observations refer to what we see or hear in the behavior of another person, while inferences consist of interpretations and conclusions we draw from what we see or hear. Observations tend to be—and to be accepted as—more objective; inferences focus on subjective interpretations. In a sense, inferences or conclusions contaminate our observations, thus clouding the feedback for another person. When inferences or conclusions *are* shared—and these data may sometimes be valuable—it is important that they be so identified.

Description, Not Judgment

When giving feedback, focus on description rather than judgment. Description simply reports what occurred, while judgment refers to an evaluation in terms of good or bad, right or wrong, nice or not nice. Judgments arise out of a personal frame of reference or values, whereas description represents neutral retelling (as far as possible). This guideline does not mean that one should not hold values but rather that the process of feedback is most productive when the aim is to report and understand, not to impose one's own values. In giving feedback, try to be a news reporter rather than to provide colorful commentary.

"More or Less," Not "Either Or"

In describing behavior, focus on "more or less," rather than "either or." "More or less" terminology suggests that a behavior falls on a continuum, that it exists in a quantity that is objective and measurable, as opposed to a quality, which is subjective and judgmental. Thus, someone's participation may fall on a continuum from low participation to high participation, rather than "good" or "bad" participation. Not to think in terms of "more or less," of continuums, is to trap ourselves into thinking in categories that may seriously distort reality. Parents often fall into this trap with children. Not recognizing growth, no matter how small, negates any effort a child has made to meet expectations.

"Here and Now," Not "There and Then"

The fifth guideline, like the fourth, refines feedback on behavior. The giver of feedback is advised to focus on comments about specific behavior in a specific situation, preferably in the "here and now," rather than on behavior in the abstract, thus removing it to the "there and then." What you and I do is always tied in some way to time and place, so we increase understanding of behavior by setting it in time and place. Feedback is generally more meaningful if it is given as soon as appropriate after the observations and reactions occur. "Here and now" keeps feedback concrete and relatively free of distortions that come with the lapse of time.

Alternatives, Not Answers

Effective feedback focuses on exploring alternatives rather than giving answers or solutions. The greater the variety of means suggested to attain a particular goal, the less likely is premature choice of a particular answer or solution—one that may not fit the problem at hand. Many of us carry around a conglomeration of ready solutions for which there are no problems.

Value to the Receiver, Not Satisfaction for the Giver

The feedback provided should serve the needs of the recipient rather than the needs of the giver. Suggestions must be spoken and heard as an offer, not an imposition, of help. The key word is "heard." Often we are eager to give feedback but fail to monitor the recipient's responses. Focus feedback on the value it may have to the receiver, not on the value or satisfaction for the person giving the feedback.

Amount of Information the Receiver Can Use

Limit feedback to the amount of information that the persons receiving it can use rather than on the amount that you might like to give. To overload a person with feedback is to reduce the possibility that the person may effectively use what is received. When we give more than can be used, we may be satisfying a need for ourselves rather than helping the other person.

Sensitivity to Time and Place

The successful giver of feedback attends to time and place when sharing personal data. Because reception of personal feedback invokes many and various emotional reactions, the giver must be sensitive to times and locations appropriate to productive feedback. Excellent feedback presented at an inappropriate time may do more harm than good.

What Is Said, Not Why

The preceding guidelines apply to the giver of feedback. However, receivers who wish to use feedback for personal growth also have responsibilities. In particular, the receiver of feedback needs to focus on *what* is being said rather than on speculation about *why* it is said. The what, how, when, and where of the feedback message are observable characteristics. The why, however, often takes us beyond the observable to the inferred and raises questions of "motive" or "intent." To make assumptions about the motives of the person giving feedback may prevent us from hearing, or cause us to distort, the message. In short, if I question "why" a person gives me feedback, I may fail to hear the feedback itself.

To sum it up, giving (and receiving) feedback requires courage, skill, understanding, and respect for self and others. Look back at the "poor" and "better" examples of feedback given above. In not one of the "poor" instances does the feedback feel good to the recipient. Pain and distress are the likely results of each of them. The difference between "poor" and "better" lies in the communication process. Each of the "poor" versions leaves the receiver with a feeling of defensiveness and suggests no clear direction in which to go. The better versions describe behavior, provide direction, and avoid attacking the person individually. When you use effective feedback skills, you increase the chances your message will be heard and acted upon. You decrease the chances that side conflicts will emerge over the style of your message, distracting attention from the content. The content should be worth fighting for; the style should not.

Negativism and Joylessness

Joyful environments are more productive than joyless ones. People get into fewer conflicts in settings they enjoy. The converse is equally true. In a highly negative, joyless environment, you become a time bomb waiting to go off. You are ripe for conflict.

Let me describe a couple of my personal terrors in life. One of them is to be in a tightly packed airplane next to a whining, crying child. This terror came true for me in 1978. All the way from Washington to Los Angeles, I had to listen to this child complain and demand and whine. By the end of the trip I was just waiting for someone to cross me. The first person who failed to do what I wanted would be the recipient of an earful of frustration. As it turned out, the methodical but nonchalant ticket-taker at the parking garage became my unsuspecting victim. On a normal day I would have said nothing; on that day, I expressed volumes of frustration.

Another of my personal terrors is to be on a Little League committee filled with hostile, negative people who want to work through their own childhood frustrations through the lives of their kids. Little League itself is wonderful. We have spent seeming centuries watching our sons play baseball, but the committee terror still exists for me. The committee members complain and moan and prattle about all the things the city will not let them do or a problem with umpires or parents' lack of concern or the laziness of the boys. In groups like this I am seldom productive—and I often say things I wish I had never uttered. Conflict abounds. Keeping things positive and proactive is one key to reducing conflict.

Conflict Traps

There are four major conflict traps: health, money, time, and clutter. People who feel unhealthy are more likely to engage in conflict than others. People experiencing money problems are more likely to fight than others. People who have, or think they have, more to do than time permits are more likely to experience conflict than others. And people in small, cluttered environments, people who feel their surroundings physically closing in on them, are more likely to look for conflicts. All of these are conflict traps because the conflicts that ensue are about side issues, not the real issues.

Take this situation, for example.

> I get up in the morning and discover I have an awful cold. I realize that my alarm has failed to go off, making me thirty minutes late. I go to take a shower and see towels and clothes everywhere. I quickly get dressed and try to leave, but my son needs money for school pictures today. I have only a twenty dollar bill, and I need that for lunch. He demands and whines, but I don't give in. He should have planned ahead, I insist. I rush to the office, but traffic is terrible. I'm closed in by cars everywhere. Finally I get to work, only to find files stacked all over my desk.

I am now ready for a productive, joyful day of work, right? Wrong! I am a time bomb waiting to happen. I am sure I will get into a fight with the first person through the door. And remember, the fight will not be about the issue of the moment; rather, it will be a by-product of the conflict traps, and any efforts to resolve the conflict will meet with limited success because they will focus on the apparent surface problem and not on the underlying conflict traps. Avoiding the traps, or at least acknowledging them openly, reduces unproductive conflict.

Mushroom Syndrome

Mushrooms grow and thrive in the dark. They feed in moist, damp, closed-in places. In the open, in the light and air, they do not do well. They shrivel and die. Many conflicts and fears fall prey to this mushroom syndrome. Small conflicts that are left unresolved, that are left unspoken and unacknowledged, often fester and grow. They grow and grow and grow until they become very large and unmanageable. Public boards are wonderful examples of this. One member may oppose the pet project of another without really understanding the sensitivity or importance of the issue. No one says anything, and things go on "rationally," but as the months and years progress, the offended member consistently votes in opposition to the ideas of his former colleague. And a feud is born.

Counselors spend hours uncovering the trivial that has become monumental. Managers spend much effort and many resources resolving conflicts that started small but somehow were never resolved at that early stage. The mushroom syndrome is pervasive and insidious. It is too easy to say, "Well, this is pretty minor; I'll let it pass. It'll go away." The trouble is, it does not go away. It just gets packed into a small, dark, damp place inside people and grows. It's much better to give small conflicts light and air. Get them out in the open!

Poor Problem Ownership

The more competent we are, the more our ego makes us think we can solve everyone else's problems. We are the saviors of others. Parents are magnificent examples of this principle. Have you ever had your child get into a big fight with a neighbor child? Your first instinct is to step in and try to resolve the conflict. Then the neighbor child's mother comes out, and *she* tries to solve "it." Before long, the two parents are engaged in a death struggle and angry words are exchanged. Meanwhile, the kids have left and are playing games together.

When you try to solve someone else's problems, you do two perilous things. First, you rob the other person of the opportunity to grow by solving his or her own problems. In your urge to be a wonderful protector, you inhibit personal responsibility and growth. Second, you increase the chances that you will become an actor in the conflict yourself. There *is* a role for you in helping others—not as savior but as consultant. You can listen, offer ideas, and reflect on possibilities. But do not become an active participant in the situation. Allow others the freedom to choose and solve for themselves. You have plenty of conflicts of your own and enough principles to do battle over. Help and support others, but do not try to solve problems for them.

Solving Before Listening

Too often, people seek to solve problems or conflicts before they have all the relevant information. They hear the surface issue and deliver an immediate response. This is the opposite of "avoidance"—it is premature strategy. The problem with this premature decision-making is not just failure to resolve the particular conflict; it is also likely that new conflicts will be created by assumption and misimpression. I am amazed at how often conflict situations consist not simply of one conflict but of a cluster of conflicts that have congealed and expanded through a series of premature "solution strategies."

I remember serving on the board of a nonprofit organization with "Solution Sal." No matter what the issue, he had something to say about it and he had a nice, neat solution. The trouble was that the board listened to him and let him have his way. One example in particular comes to mind. We needed a new building, so Sal convinced the board that all the money could be raised through small individual donations and sales of commemorative plaques. They tried it without really examining the process of fund-raising or researching the interest of local residents. The project failed, and Sal chided everyone else for lack of commitment. Many hurt feelings, as well as a general perception that our organization was pretty inept, resulted from this premature venture into fund-raising.

To solve conflict effectively you need to understand the problem and know the range of solutions and their consequences. Diagnosis must precede prescription. There is the old joke of the guy who goes to the doctor and says, "My arm hurts when I do this," to which the doctor replies, "Then don't do it." You cannot have the right solution until you know the real cause of the pain, the real cause of the conflict.

"Last Tags" Complex

We often find great truths in cartoons and jokes. In this case, we are reminded of a panel of cartoons in *Mad Magazine* showing two antagonists who shared a longtime, deep-seated rivalry. One is on his deathbed, and he summons the other. The first man signals his lifelong foe to come closer and closer to hear his faint, last words. The dying man suddenly leans upward toward his rival, proclaims "Last tags!" and dies. This is the ultimate "last tags," the ultimate one-upmanship. Many of us spend our lives trying to get the last word, the last idea, the last victory. We are not content until we are secure in "last tags." Living and working with people like that is very difficult. Everything is a competition, the point being to top the other person rather than simply to fulfill one's own needs. People who live lives of "last tags" also live lives of conflict and tension and discomfort.

I remember when I was off to an elite prep school as a child to make my way in the world. I was relatively poor, having grown up in a rural farm community, and I was eager to please. On my first day in school, I ran into a bunch of seniors. I was a twelve-year-old eighth-grader, probably the consummate country bumpkin. These seniors decided to have some fun with me, so they picked me up, put me in a full-length locker, and locked me inside—*for eight hours*! *I* went through various stages of despair . . . disbelief . . . panic . . . terror . . . and ultimately resolve. This resolve was that I would never let anyone do that to me again. I was going to be harder and tougher and more sarcastic than anyone else. After my release, I was true to my resolve and I lived out my early years in a world of competition and "last tags." I believe I am now beyond that, but the point is that all of us have our own locker stories. Only to the degree to which we can progress beyond the resolve made in the "locker" can we effectively manage conflicts. Only to that degree can we avoid creating new dissension out of our need to best the bullies of our past.

Scenario Analysis

These, then, are the nine pollutants that choke the climate for effective resolution of organizational conflicts. Which of them was at work in the scenario of lights on the football field? There were several. We suggest that you analyze this case on your own first, using table 4.3, and then refer to table 4.4 and the following paragraphs for our analysis.

We found three major pollutants present in that scenario and three lesser ones. The biggest single problem we saw was the simplistic and unjustified expectation that in face of a fiscal crisis, lights for a playing field held the highest priority. Even if this had been an important issue, the boosters unrealistically expected the board to appropriate the money or—just as unrealistic—expected potlucks and candy sales to generate $100,000. They were not clear about fiscal realities. They expected too much.

Second, they did little to articulate the principles that were operating

Table 4.3. Assessment of Conflict Pollutants

	Not at all		Somewhat		To a great degree
1. Preferences above principles	1	2	3	4	5
2. Undue expectations	1	2	3	4	5
3. Poor feedback skills	1	2	3	4	5
4. Negativism/joylessness	1	2	3	4	5
5. Conflict traps					
a. Health	1	2	3	4	5
b. Money	1	2	3	4	5
c. Time	1	2	3	4	5
d. Clutter	1	2	3	4	5
6. Mushroom syndrome	1	2	3	4	5
7. Poor problem ownership	1	2	3	4	5
8. Premature solution	1	2	3	4	5
9. "Last tags" complex	1	2	3	4	5

Table 4.4. Conflict Pollutants Assessment (Dwight Eisenhower High School)

	Not at all		Somewhat		To a great degree
1. Preferences above principles	1	2	3	**4**	5
2. Undue expectations	1	2	3	4	**5**
3. Poor feedback skills	1	**2**	3	4	5
4. Negativism/joylessness	1	2	**3**	4	5
5. Conflict traps					
a. Health	**1**	2	3	4	5
b. Money	1	2	3	**4**	5
c. Time	1	2	3	**4**	5
d. Clutter	**1**	2	3	4	5
6. Mushroom syndrome	1	2	**3**	4	5
7. Poor problem ownership	**1**	2	3	4	5
8. Premature solution	1	2	**3**	4	5
9. "Last tags" complex	1	**2**	3	4	5

Selected values in bold

in their minds. They had a preference for night football games. What is the key educational principle at work? Perhaps there was one, but no one ever really argued it. The boosters expected everyone to embrace their preference. They argued preference above principle.

Third, and most obviously, there was a fiscal shortage. In the face of tight money, the situation became very strident. The conflict trap of money came into play. The short time line, another conflict trap, exacerbated the problem.

Other lesser factors were the continued complaints and negativism of the group. In this case the board was "fed up" with the constant whining of the booster group. The board had grown callous to the boosters' concern. Negativism and joylessness took over.

Lastly, there was paradoxical interaction of pollutants. On the one hand, Mike was hoping the problem would go away; he thought the candy sale strategy would work. The problem was already bad enough at that point, but a premature—and unsuitable—solution that ignored the problem's underlying roots only allowed time for the problem to grow. On the other hand, Mike knew the solution would not be easy. He saw the complexity of the dilemma and its potential to become a major, long-term problem. He just hoped he was wrong. Like the superintendent who did nothing until his board member pulled a gun, Mike acted on his hope for peace, rather than on his own best judgment. Failure to confront conflict does not bring peace; it just builds bigger conflicts.

TYPES OF CONFLICT

Conflict pollutants constitute the first domain of managing conflict. The second component deals with the five types of conflict. This section, the shortest in this chapter, is nevertheless the most important. This is true because the single greatest error in conflict management is failure to match an appropriate resolution strategy to a particular type of conflict. Conflict is not of one kind, but the literature often assumes it is. Even when writers recognize multiple types of conflict, they often focus on the categories of "intergroup," "interorganizational," and "interpersonal" conflict. We find that this differentiation is not very useful to managers (Rahim 1986). We do not contest the theory, simply its utility in practical applications.

We contend that the following differentiation is far more useful in managing the realities of conflict than the three-way classification just mentioned. The five types of conflict, then, are:

1. Value conflicts
2. Tangible conflicts
3. Interpersonal conflicts
4. Boundary conflicts
5. Perceptual conflicts

Each will be considered in turn.

Value Conflicts

Value conflicts are struggles over beliefs, tenets, or principles. They often involve convictions held on faith, independent of evidence or logic. They evolve from the history of the individual or the experiences of the group. As a school principal, I encountered many situations that were rooted in value conflicts. A frequent example was the parents who came to complain about a consequence given to their child for fighting. Often the child had reacted after being hit by another youngster. The school rules were quite clear: Fighting, regardless of who started it, was still fighting. The school valued total absence of fighting. The parents who came to see me, however, valued self-defense. Our belief systems were in opposition; therefore, a value conflict existed.

Value conflicts are not readily solved; indeed, in most cases they cannot be resolved. Differing parties simply learn to coexist within an understanding or appreciation of their fundamental differences. Examples of value conflicts are differences between parties relative to:

- Teaching versus research
- Profit-making versus social responsibility
- Pacifism versus confronting the enemy
- Work versus family
- Individual versus group needs
- Academic versus nonacademic needs
- Obedience versus individualism

These are just a few examples of value differences that can emerge in conflict situations. The list could go on and on and on.

Tangible Conflicts

Tangible conflicts are those that arise over elements that can be measured, divided, counted, or shared. Money is a classic area of tangible conflict. We do not have enough money to do everything we want, so we conflict over priorities in expending available dollars. Other tangible conflicts may concern time, facilities, personnel, benefits, and the like. Tangible conflicts tend to fall in the resource domain and, in reality, are more readily resolved than the other types. The problem with them, however, is that we tend to misdiagnose them or take simplistic authoritative command approaches to their resolution. In so doing, we only make them worse. Whenever conflicts can be handled at the tangible level, do so. Specific strategies are described later in this chapter.

Interpersonal Conflicts

Interpersonal conflicts arise from my feelings about you as a person. "I've never liked you" or "I've never liked that quality in you" are common mental scripts. Interpersonal conflicts are very common in organizations and are the second most difficult to resolve (value conflicts are the toughest). The most important thing to remember about an interpersonal conflict is that it is very seldom the progenitor conflict. It is very seldom the initiating issue; rather, it is typically a secondary result of some other conflict.

Let me illustrate this with a story. Imagine a seventh-grade boy emerging from his room wearing a grungy, dirty T-shirt. His mother is appalled and the following interchange ensues:

Mother: "Mark, don't you have any other shirts?"
Son: "Yeah. (Looking down at his shirt.) But this one is fine. I like it the way it is."
Mother: "Mark, I do the wash for you so that you will have clean shirts. What will your teachers think of me?"
Son: "I don't know, but *all* the kids wear shirts like this. It's okay."
Mother: "No it's not! How many times have I told you to wear clean clothes to school? You *never* listen to me. Don't you care what I tell you? Don't you care about me?"
Son: "Get off my case! I'm the one at school all day."
Mother: "Change it now!"

Mark returns to his room and slams the door. Later, he unhappily returns with a clean T-shirt and a high level of frustration. Was the conflict resolved? Perhaps the immediate issue was resolved, but it will return in larger form later and later and later. The mother originally assumed that the conflict was of the tangible type—whether or not Mark had clean shirts. When that turned out not to be the issue, she tried to make it interpersonal—"Don't you care about me?" In reality, the contest involved a values conflict. Mother values cleanliness; Mark values fitting into the peer culture.

When you misdiagnose the type of conflict, you cannot select an appropriate strategy, and you often escalate one conflict into an entire cluster of controversies. What was once a value conflict now becomes two conflicts—one over values, the other over interpersonal caring. As in this story, interpersonal conflict is seldom the original conflict; it is usually a by-product of some other conflict that has been misdiagnosed or inadequately resolved. When you see an interpersonal conflict, look for the presence of some other conflict also. In most cases you will find one.

Boundary Conflicts

Boundary conflicts are of two kinds—boundary penetration and boundary expansion. In the first case, you believe you have a certain territory, area, or role that is yours and someone has violated it. For instance, you think it is your job to make decisions about monetary expenditures and then find that someone else has gone ahead and made decisions without you. You are angry because your role, your domain, has been preempted. Someone has penetrated into your realm. Or, to take a more concrete example, you may have an office that is your own. How would you feel if you now had to share it with someone else? Boundary penetrations are among the most common conflicts we have and also are most likely to fall prey to the mushroom syndrome described earlier.

The second kind of conflict in this category is boundary expansion. I am expecting you to step in and help when someone is sick or absent, but you don't see that as your job. The problem is that I want you to expand your role boundaries and you do not want to. The classic Freddie Prinze line comes to mind here: "It's not my job, man."

Both these boundary conflicts are common. They fall somewhere in the middle of the spectrum of resolution difficulty. But left unresolved, they frequently lead to interpersonal conflicts.

Perceptual Conflicts

Perceptual conflicts are the easiest to resolve. They revolve around mutual misunderstanding. "I didn't realize that" is a phrase often heard as perceptual conflicts are resolved. Perceptual conflicts are rife on school campuses. Most parent–teacher conflicts lie in the perceptual arena. Since parents cannot be present at all times, they must rely on the word of their child as to what is happening at school.

Suppose that a student carries home a tale of too much homework. The child uses family time to complete it, and the parents become upset. An angry visit to the school results in the teacher carefully outlining the time given to complete the assignment in class in order to minimize work to be completed at home. (And often the work had been assigned several days or weeks earlier, as well!) With this new information, the parents have a different perception of the teacher's assignments, and the conflict is resolved. Of course, a parent–child conflict may just be beginning.

Perceptual conflicts evolve out of failure to communicate or, when communicating, to give adequate information. Because they are the easiest to resolve, most people like to believe that perceptual conflicts are also the most common—but they are not. If they were, conflict management would be a relatively easy, informational task. However, mere information is seldom sufficient to resolve a conflict—even though we wish it were so.

Case Analysis

Given this differentiation of conflicts, what type of conflict do we have in the scenario about the Dwight Eisenhower school board and the school's booster club? This was clearly a conflict over money. If the school board had had enough money, it would have replaced the lights for the football field. However, underlying all this activity was an unarticulated value conflict about the importance of football versus other activities. It quickly became interpersonal, relative to both the board ("recall") and Mike ("Are you with us or against us?"). Had the tangible conflict been addressed more effectively early on, and had the value conflict been articulated openly, the more difficult interpersonal conflict might never have evolved. A latent issue that developed subsequently was the board's role in expanding district resources. This was a boundary issue—boundary expansion from the perspective of the boosters; boundary penetration from the position of the board. Finally, note that Mike hoped this was a perceptual issue, and that his explanation of the problems facing the district would cause the conflict to dissipate. It did not. It just got bigger.

CONFLICT RESOLUTION STRATEGIES

Once you know the type of conflict you face, you need to determine an appropriate strategy. We propose thirteen basic conflict resolution strategies (see table 4.5), each with a different degree of effectiveness relative to each type of conflict. We will briefly describe the thirteen strategies and then suggest the utility of each.

Problem-Solving

Problem-solving is undoubtedly the most-used strategy for managing and resolving conflicts. Filley (1975), Rahim (1986), Carpenter and Kennedy (1988), and Blake and Mouton (1984) all use some variation of problem-solving to tackle organizational disputes. Problem-solving starts with the assumption that you must carefully define the nature of the problem, search for an array of solutions through a variety of data-gathering approaches, and then, through consensus, choose a mutually acceptable alternative. This is classic problem-solving. We wish to propose two problem-solving models as particularly useful in conflict management: Filley's Integrative Decision-Making Model (IDM) and Harvey's Directive Collaboration Model (DCM).

Filley's Integrative Decision-Making Model (IDM)

Table 4.6 presents Filley's model (Filley 1975). You will note that it contains three important initial steps that precede classic problem-solving. These steps have been added to the classic model because Filley's is fundamentally a conflict resolution strategy. As such, it recognizes

---

Table 4.5.   Conflict Resolution Strategies

1. Problem-solving
2. Expansion of resources
3. Establishing a superordinate goal
4. Interdependence analysis
5. Compromise
6. Authoritative command
7. Organizational structure alteration
8. Human-relations interventions
9. Third-party intervention
10. Role-analysis technique
11. Norm-setting
12. Communication and feedback
13. Smoothing and avoidance

Table 4.6.   Integrative Decision-Making (IDM): A Problem-Solving Approach

1. Review and adjust relational conditions
   - Examine process for communication and trust levels

2. Review and adjust perceptions
   - Avoid hidden agendas
   - Discuss grievances

3. Review and adjust attitudes
   - Review importance of eight attitudes

4. Define the problem
   - Be clear about what is to be achieved by solution
   - Generate solution criteria

5. Search for solutions
   - Use brainstorming, surveys, discussion groups—all can help generate solutions. Don't pick one at this point!

6. Make a consensus-based decision
   - Examine the full range of solutions
   - Evaluate solutions for quality and acceptability
   - Avoid a defensive environment
   - Avoid voting, flipping coins, averaging
   - Focus on agreement with criteria

7. Set up a system to monitor the implementation of the solution
   - Determine who
   - Determine when

Source: A. Filley, *Interpersonal Conflict Resolution* (Glenview, IL: Scott Foresman, 1975).

that almost always, one must deal with feelings and expectations before proceeding along a rational problem-solving path.

The first step—review and adjust relational conditions—responds to the need for a trusting relationship among the parties and acknowledges interpersonal associations as a basis for resolving organizational disputes. The second step—review and adjust perceptions—seeks to uncover any hidden agendas or past grudges and grievances. Phrases such as "This will never work" or "We've done this before, and no one has ever listened" are typical at this point. It is important to bring these doubts to the surface. If you do not, they will surely sabotage your process. In the open, they are less dangerous.

The third step—review and adjust attitudes—explores beliefs and attitudes that undergird the process. Beliefs conducive to the IDM model include the following eight attitudes:

- Belief in the availability of a mutually acceptable solution
- Belief in the desirability of a mutually acceptable solution
- Belief in cooperation rather than competition
- Belief that everyone is of worth in decision-making
- Belief in the views of others as legitimate statements of their position
- Belief that differences of opinion are helpful
- Belief in the trustworthiness of other members coupled with a risk-giving trust on the part of each participant
- Belief that the other party could compete but chooses to cooperate

A set of operational beliefs to govern the process of decision-making, beliefs similar to those just listed, is essential to the IDM. They act much like the norms discussed in chapter 3. The rest of the Integrative Decision-Making model proceeds much like any problem-solving model.

Harvey's Directive Collaboration Model (DCM)

A second problem-solving model is Harvey's Directive Collaboration Model (Harvey 1990). It assumes that in a highly charged, low-trust environment, purely collaborative problem-solving will not work. Step numbers 1, 2, 3, 7, 8, 11, and 13 in this model reflect Filley's basic approach, but the other steps add a directive dimension to the process of problem-solving as a conflict resolution strategy. These are added because:

- In volatile environments you need to be directive at some points and highly collaborative at others. You need to control the process of defining the problem, the time line for its solution, and constraints and unacceptable outcomes. Otherwise the decision-making process will likely be deflected into side issues or avoided and defocused.
- To keep the process effective and rational, you need to blend active participation on the part of the affected partners with expertise and data-gathering. If you have only participation, you are simply pooling collective ignorance; if you have only expertise, the group

may seem to act rationally yet lack personal commitment to the solution.

For fuller exploration of each model, we refer you to the sources for tables 4.6 and 4.7; here we have had space only to mention the key steps and assumptions. We also do not intend that you limit consideration of problem-solving to these particular models. Filley's IDM and Harvey's DCM are simply two models we have found particularly useful.

Problem-solving is indeed a very effective strategy for resolving some conflicts. It is not useful, however, in all arenas. For instance, problem-solving is particularly appropriate for tangible conflicts because these involve properties that can be measured and divided and hence are subject to rational analysis. Problem-solving is particularly ineffective, however, for value conflicts because beliefs and faith are not the domain of logical discourse or evidence. Problem-solving approaches in the face of such debates as pro-life versus pro-choice wither and fail. No one strategy works all the time; rather, different strategies are appropriate to different types of conflict. If you consistently use one strategy, you will be right part of the time and wrong most of the time. Problem-solving approaches are extremely useful, but far from sufficient.

Table 4.7.   Directive Collaboration Model (DCM): A Problem-Solving Approach

C	1. Include all sides
C	2. Establish collaborative norms/processes
D	3. Define problem domain/decision set
D	4. Define time frame
D	5. Define givens (political, budgetary, etc.)
D	6. Define unacceptable outcomes
C	7. Reinvent part of a wheel
C	8. Reach for consensus
D	9. Use systematic decision processes
D	10. Use expertise at appropriate points
C	11. Monitor/debrief process
C	12. Discuss drafts
C	13. Emphasize group credit/accountability

C = Collaborative step
D = Directive step
Source: Thomas Harvey, *Checklist for Change* (Needham, MA: Allyn & Bacon, 1990).

Expansion of Resources

Consider two children fighting over the same toy. One way to resolve their dispute is to give each child the identical toy. This tactic is essentially the expansion of resources strategy—when legitimate demands are greater than the resources at hand, simply expand or enhance the resources. This is a delightful, satisfying approach in resource-rich environments.

The 1960s was such a decade. Real family income increased significantly, and we enjoyed a wonderfully extravagant era in which one simply demonstrated a project as "good" and the nation supported it— whether you were touting national defense, social services, education, health care, civil rights, or putting a man on the moon. In more recent decades, we have not been as lucky. We now live in a post-extravagant era in which we must ask ourselves whether something is "better," not just "good." Is child care better than elder care? Is education better than health care? Is national defense better than social services? These are difficult comparisons none of us wish to make, but often we must. Ours is a resource-scarce time; hence, expansion of resources has limited utility at the moment.

The reason for including this strategy, despite its limitations, is two-fold. First, many managers in positions of leadership today grew up in those resource-rich days. They have a strong mental disposition to resolve conflict simply by adding more people, facilities, time, or money. And they are deeply frustrated when they cannot. Thus, they must understand the drawbacks to resource expansion. Second, you will encounter a popular inclination to expand resources, particularly in public disputes involving elected bodies or policy issues. You need more police? Just get more money to hire them. Need to refurbish a school? Simply pass a bond issue to do it. Want to reduce smog? Demand car pooling by everyone. The public has little inclination to give more resources, yet it believes that your job is to expand resources in the face of conflicting needs. If resources can be expanded, expand them! But if, as is far more likely, that cannot be done, be prepared to fend off this approach as a "quick fix" method for resolving a conflict of priorities.

Nevertheless, remember that in resource-scarce times, there may yet be creative alternatives, entrepreneurial solutions, that do not add resources per se but reuse them to derive greater benefit for more people. The scenario of the conflict over the lights for the football field was a case in which a school district and a city shared facilities to increase their use. Time was expanded so that existing space could be used more effectively.

Superordinate Goal

Using the superordinate goal is a strategy that appeals to a higher-order belief or value. A common superordinate goal in a conflict-filled union is "We need to hang together if we expect to get a raise," or in a hospital you might hear "We are all in this for the sake of the patient." These are values, beliefs, or goals that overarch the conflict of the moment. This strategy is particularly effective in value conflicts when

- There are higher values than those under dispute.
- All parties in the dispute have a commonly held higher value.

If either of these conditions is *not* met, then the strategy of appealing to the superordinate goal cannot work. If the subject of a given conflict involves the highest belief held by one or more of the parties, then no superordinate goal is there. This situation most often arises in religious or moral disputes. Similarly, if each party holds different values, then the parties cannot come to agreement. For management, the highest value may be creation of profit or social responsibility; for the union, it may be protection of the rights of workers or betterment of the lives of individuals. All are higher goals, but they are different. Appealing to the superordinate goal is a reasonable and productive strategy, but it works best with value conflicts where the two conditions pertain.

Interdependence Analysis

Interdependence analysis works much like the superordinate goal in that it seeks to establish mutual acceptance by appealing to a higher reality. Superordinate goals can be referenced to appeal to a higher value; interdependence analysis builds on the mutual need we have for one another. "I need you and you need me. We must resolve this because we'll hurt each other too much if we don't." When two or more parties in a dispute truly understand that their interests are interdependent and that they need each other for future success, a basis exists for exploring alternatives and reaching agreements. Only when I feel that I can get along nicely without you do I act capriciously or callously. Table 4.8 describes the steps in an exercise called Interdependence Analysis. This procedure is useful in clarifying mutuality of need. You will note that this exercise does not directly attack the content of the dispute but rather establishes an environment conducive for reaching agreement. This approach, which is often combined with other strategies, is particularly appropriate for interpersonal, value, and boundary conflicts.

Compromise

Compromise is one of the more common approaches to conflict management. You give up half a loaf, I'll give up half a loaf, and we will be even. This is the theory of mutual deprivation—one agrees as long as the other party is equally deprived. This strategy works well as long as the dispute entails moderately important goals. On the other hand, if the conflict involves a critical organizational issue, compromise gives up too much—someone loses a *full* loaf in the process. In such cases, we should strive to gain as much as possible rather than to settle for compromise or mutual deprivation.

Compromise assumes equal power. A supervisor and employee have difficulty compromising—the supervisor holds all the power. Where parties have unequal power, power must somehow be relatively equalized before compromise works. Another condition under which com-

---

Table 4.8. Steps in Interdependence Analysis

1. Whom do you need to get your job done?
2. To what degree and for what do you need each of these people?
3. Who needs you to get their job done?
4. To what degree and for what do they need you?
5. Do the answers to steps 1 and 2 match the answers to steps 3 and 4?
6. How do your perceptions compare with those of colleagues?

promise works well is an occasion that calls for a temporary settlement with a more comprehensive resolution to follow later. Compromise works well as an intermediate solution.

Authoritative Command

Authoritative command is one of the most appealing and time-efficient strategies we have. "Do it because I told you to do it!" Authoritative command is the typical response to the classic case of two children squabbling over shared toys. The authoritative response sounds like: "You take this toy and you take that one; now *stop* fighting."

The trouble with authoritative command is that it creates little investment in the solution. If I do not participate in designing a resolution, I have little commitment to maintaining it. The authoritative approach also creates win-lose outcomes—or even lose-lose outcomes. When this happens, a new enemy is created—*you*. You move from the role of helper in the present conflict situation to combatant in a new one.

Another dilemma created by using authoritative command is that it leaves the parties without skills to resolve subsequent disputes. The authority figure, acting as a deus ex machina, fails to expand the conflict resolution skills of the organizational members, who consequently become increasingly dependent on "divine authority."

Authoritative command is appropriate under two conditions:

- when speed of response and resolution are critical—perhaps due to short time lines or safety issues
- when authority is acceptable to the people involved—For example, an army sergeant is more likely to accept authoritative command than a high school teacher

Where there is a narrow span of acceptance or time is not a critical issue, other strategies should be employed.

Organizational Structure Alteration

You are a supervisor and you have two employees who complain that the other is distracting. What do you do? You partition off their office space. This is altering the organizational structure. Other examples occur when you:

- Transfer an employee to another part of the organization
- Fire an employee
- Change job roles so two secretaries need not work together
- Change the reporting structure
- Create a new organizational chart

These examples all illustrate how one can alter the organizational structure to eliminate interaction between disputing parties. Changing the structure of an organization is a common strategy, but it has some drawbacks:

- You may lose some talented people who are hard to replace.
- Training new personnel will increase costs.
- You may simply shift the problem to another department.
- You may relieve the symptom but miss the underlying problem.

If none of these drawbacks pertains to your situation, then alteration of the organizational structure can be efficient and productive.

Human Relations Interventions

   A resistance we have recurrently encountered as consultants entering organizations to help them resolve their conflicts is fear among organization members that we will get into "that touchy-feely stuff." They are afraid we may elicit emotions that burgeon out of control and become distractive and hurtful. Personal vulnerability is a great concern—in many ways a thoroughly legitimate one. However, a number of human relations interventions are available that, properly handled, improve human function without damaging personal psyches (see table 4.9).

   All of these require a long-term commitment to gradual increase in understanding and sensitivity. Not generally productive for urgent, volatile, short-term conflicts, these interventions work much better in retreat settings or as process approaches while pursuing other legiti-

Table 4.9.   Human Relations Interventions

1. Sensitivity sessions
2. Feeling awareness activities
3. Trust formation
4. Team building
5. Power awareness
6. Values clarification
7. Airing of grievances (informal)
8. Questioning strategy
9. Multicultural awareness
10. Cooperative learning approaches

mate organizational activities, such as strategic planning or program evaluation or budgeting.

Another problem you may encounter is lack of familiarity with structuring such a process. To aid the reader in this, we suggest the University Associates (now Pfeiffer and Co.) material, particularly the twenty years of Annual Handbooks for Group Facilitators as well as the multiple volumes of structured experiences for group facilitators. These handbooks are an immeasurably valuable resource.

Third-Party Intervention

Third-party intervention is another common and useful strategy for conflict resolution. It may be used by itself or in combination with other strategies. Third-party intervention involves exactly what its name implies: introduction of a third or outside person into a conflict to facilitate its resolution. There are four levels of potential third parties: facilitators, negotiators, arbitrators, and interveners (table 4.10).

1. *Facilitator.* As a facilitator, the third party seeks to clarify the nature of the problem and to elicit ideas and feelings from the disputants. The facilitator often paraphrases and questions the positions of the disputants but always with the intent that they remain in charge of their own solution. The purpose is to elevate the quality of the analysis and potential solutions. A counselor serves such a role.

Table 4.10.   Third-Party Intervention

Facilitators	Arbitrators
• Clarify	• Arbitrate
• Elicit	• Offer fixed solutions (choose one way or other)
• Paraphrase	• Offer flextble solutions (create alternatives)
• Elevate quality of analysis and solutions	• Make decisions
	• Make rulings
	• Construct action plans

Negotiators	Interveners
• Mediate	• Impose solutions
• Equalize power or outcomes	• Initiate action
• Provide options	

2. *Negotiator.* As a negotiator, the third party takes a stronger role than that of facilitator. The negotiator mediates differences and forces clarification. This role is designed to equalize power between the disputants by actively providing options and delivering judgments to accomplish a just resolution. While this is an active role, the negotiator recognizes that the solution is still in the hands of the disputants. Negotiating, in this sense, is similar to mediation.

3. *Arbitrator.* As an arbitrator, the third party has been selected by the disputants to make a decision. This role is stronger than the previous two. In deciding, an arbitrator can pursue either fixed arbitration (as in arbitration of baseball salaries, where the arbitrator picks one position or the other) or flexible arbitration (in which the third party creates new alternatives, as in binding arbitration in school districts). In either form, parties seek a ruling and a statement describing what they are to do to.

4. *Intervener.* An intervener enters disputes independently. The disputants have not invited the intervener and often do not welcome the intrusion. In this role, the intervener, who initiates all the action, examines the data and imposes solutions. The principal who breaks up a fight between two kids is an intervener, as is a court-appointed trustee who takes control of a bankrupt organization.

All four of these roles have utility in conflict situations. We suggest, however, that the more you use the latter two roles (arbitrator or intervener), the more toxic your organization and the more subsequent conflicts you are likely to breed. On the other hand, the more you rely on the first two roles (facilitator or negotiator), the more control internal members retain and the more investment they maintain in the outcome.

Role-Analysis Technique (RAT)

The role-analysis technique is an excellent strategy for resolving boundary conflicts. It involves the clarification and adaptation of individual organizational roles (Huse 1975). Table 4.11 describes the steps involved in a RAT (also referred to as Job Expectation Technique, or JET). Perhaps it would help to recount how we handled this in a conflict situation. We had a case of two administrative aides in the same office who were constantly in disputes with each other. One had been there a long time; the other was relatively new, having been there a year or so.

Step 1: We discussed the nature of the conflicts they were encountering and determined that they were angry because each was invading the job responsibilities of the other. In some cases, a job was

Table 4.11. Role Analysis Technique (RAT)

1. Analyze conflict situation for appropriateness of RAT.
2. Establish purposes of RAT.
3. Select place and commit time.
4. Define job expectations for role being discussed—brainstorm phase.
   - Individual defines own role expectations
   - Individual adds role functions and expectations
   - Individual drops role functions and expectations
   - Group adds functions and expectations
   - Group drops functions and expectations
5. Create a consensus about job expectations.
   - Group reaches consensus
   - Individual writes own job description
   - Description is distributed
6. Repeat process for each individual.
7. Do periodic reality checks.

Source: Huse 1975.

also left undone because each thought it was the task responsibility of the other.

Step 2: We described the RAT and obtained their agreement to do it.

Step 3: We selected a time frame (1.5 hours) and setting (staff meeting of six people) to perform the RAT.

Step 4: At the subsequent meeting we asked Alice to describe her job. We recorded this on chart paper for all to see. Alice was then invited to add or drop functions from her list. We then encouraged the total group to add other things they expected of her. We also asked them to suggest tasks and functions to be dropped.

Step 5: With all these expectations in the open, we helped the group create a shared, explicit understanding of Alice's role in the organization. When the group reached consensus, we asked Alice to write a description of her role to bring back to the group in one week.

Step 6: We then repeated the entire process for Mike, the other administrative aide.

Step 7: When the cycle had been completed for both Alice and Mike, we asked the group whether the two roles now made sense in relationship to one another. We tried out some crisis scenarios to see whether everyone had the same understanding of the roles.

The RAT is not a particularly complex notion, but it does provide a structured mechanism for clarifying roles and boundaries. Most of us are given a job description (which is often outdated) on our first day of work and that is the last time we systematically record what we are to do as a worker. But jobs change, and roles change with them. We expect that somehow workers will "discover" their new roles and do them extraordinarily well. In some cases, we are correct; in most cases, we are not. It is small wonder that one of the most common areas of conflict is the boundary dispute.

Norm-Setting

As explained in an earlier chapter, norm-setting is a powerful management tool that should be incorporated into all organizational settings. However, conflicts often arise for which you have not generated any norms or in organizations where no explicit norms exist at all. In fact, the conflict has arisen precisely *because* no norms exist. The strategy then calls for generating norms in the midst of the conflict.

By its very nature, norm-setting can turn an irrational situation into a more rational, focused conflict resolution session as opposing parties come to agreement. A norm is an operational principle or expectation that implicitly or explicitly governs the actions of a group of people. The process of defining norms deflects immediate discussion from the "what," or content of the conflict, to the more objective "how," or the procedures to be followed. It shifts the focus from laying blame for past errors to establishing guidelines for future behavior. Without these guidelines, participants are left to their individual rules of behavior, rules that are often in opposition. While other conflict management strategies are often over-used, norm-setting is an underused—but often successful—strategy for conflict resolution, particularly for interpersonal and boundary conflicts.

I remember the case of two long-time co-workers who literally had not spoken to each other in two years. They were the only two professionals in the office, and they set the tone for a highly toxic, suspicion-ridden environment. It was not my job to make them friends but rather to establish some guidelines for behavior. The norms we established were as follows:

Over the next six months we will:

- Be interpersonally civil in the office
- Meet weekly with each other to discuss issues, problems, and successes
- Find appropriate times and places for feedback (both positive and negative)
- Meet face to face as much as possible (a moratorium on memos)
- Ask each other about our concerns—no mind-reading, no assumptions
- Pose fewer accusatory questions
- Avoid end runs—via memo or orally
- Involve each other in decisions that affect us both

Other norms could have just as easily been set. The essential element is the process itself, not the content of the norms themselves. A similar procedure could also have been applied to conflicts over boundary penetration or expansion. Norm-setting is a versatile and useful approach to conflict management.

Communication and Feedback

Communication and feedback is a much overused strategy. A disputant often assumes that another person disagrees with her simply because she does not understand. "If only he knew the situation better," "If only he knew reality," "If only he knew me"—then, we are certain, he would agree. We readily assume that most conflicts are perceptual, but they are not.

Just recently we were asked to organize a management retreat to help an organization address its "communication" problems. When we talked with the participants, we found that middle managers wanted more control and felt they were ignored too often. They had complained about this but had been rebuffed. When we talked with upper management, we found they were well aware of the requests for greater involvement but felt that middle managers were overstepping their bounds. The problem here was not communication. A clear message had already been sent and received. Rather, the recipients did not like the content of the messages. The issue was penetration of upper management's boundary for decision-making. The conflict would not be resolved without addressing that underlying issue.

Communication and feedback do help when a conflict originates in misunderstanding. This strategy is also useful in combination with others. But be careful not to rely on it unduly.

Smoothing and Avoidance

Because they are the least desirable among conflict-management strategies, smoothing and avoidance have been left to last. While they work at times, they are probably the most overused of strategies. The meaning of avoidance strategy is obvious—I simply close my eyes and hope the problem will go away. The trouble is, that often does not happen. Instead, the conflict goes underground and illustrates the mushroom syndrome—it gets larger and larger.

Smoothing, on the other hand, is the process of comforting everyone in the midst of the dispute. "We don't really disagree on this." "We're a lot closer than we think." "This is really not that important to fight over." Smoothing is much like my behavior as a child when my mother served me peas. I would smash them down and spread them all over the plate. I would then look at her saying, "See, Mom, the peas are all gone." But they were not—and she knew it. The same is true of most conflicts. We may think we have done away with them by smoothing them out, but typically they re-emerge later.

However, avoidance and smoothing work on some occasions. These are times when

- The issue is truly trivial, a product of the immediate moment.
- The timing is wrong for any other strategy. For example, consider a hostile citizen at a public meeting. The best approach may be to smooth things over until a later time when the city manager can deal with the substantive issue more directly.
- The issue can be resolved by someone else. You need not solve every problem you encounter.
- You are in the midst of other, more critical conflict situations. You cannot do everything at once and may need to defer a conflict until other matters have been settled.

Be careful to use avoidance and smoothing only when such conditions exist.

MATCHING STRATEGIES WITH CONFLICTS

We find the thirteen conflict-resolution strategies just discussed the most effective in resolving organizational disputes. Table 4.12 presents the relationship between types of conflict discussed earlier and the several resolution strategies. For value conflicts, preferable strategies are appeals to the superordinate goal and interdependence analysis. For tangible conflicts, we prefer problem-solving, expansion of resources, and alteration of the organizational structure. For interpersonal conflicts, we incline toward norm-setting, interdependence analysis, and

Table 4.12. Relevance of Strategies to Conflict Types

Conflict-Resolution Strategy	Type of Conflict				
	Value Conflict	Tangible Conflict	Inter-personal Conflict	Boundary Expansion/ Penetration	Perceptual Conflict
Problem-solving		1*		1*	
Expansion of resources		2*		2	
Superordinate goal	3*		3		
Interdependence analysis	4*		4*	4	
Compromise	5	5		5	
Authoritative command	6	6	6	6	
Alteration of organizational structure	7	7*	7	7	
Human relations interventions			8*		8
Third-party intervention	9	9	9	9*	
Role analysis technique				10*	
Norm-setting			11*	11*	11*
Communication and feedback			12	12	12*
Smoothing and avoidance	13		13		

*Preferred values

human relations interventions. For boundary conflicts, our preferred approaches are role analysis technique, norm-setting, and third-party intervention. Finally, for perceptual conflict, our preferred strategies are norm-setting and communication and feedback.

Case Analysis

Let us illustrate the application of these strategies by returning to the lights-for-the-football-field scenario. As described earlier, this was initially, and primarily, a tangible conflict—there was not enough money to do everything. A value conflict was also involved. How was the situation actually handled? We recommended that at the next board meeting, when Jim Sykes and the boosters voiced their unhappiness, Superintendent Murray acknowledge them and encourage the board president to allow time for them to voice their concerns. She would then lead them to clarify their values and subsequently recommend a task force including the boosters and school personnel to seek a resolution to the conflicting demands. We recommended a directive collaboration approach and suggested that she give the group a three-month time line. She did all this, and the boosters responded positively. We also suggested that the meeting be conducted in such a way as to remedy some of the interpersonal wounds that had been inflicted. The group eventually returned with a recommendation to work with the city, which would pay for the lights in return for use of the field at off-school times. (This strategy should sound familiar; it is the one we also referred to as an example of the expansion of resources.) This alternative worked, and everyone was satisfied.

This scenario illustrates the need to analyze conflict systematically and resolve it with appropriate strategies. At the end of this chapter, we have included several other cases for your consideration. We suggest that you analyze each, select a strategy or combination of strategies from table 4.12, and then refer to our suggestion.

MANAGEMENT OF DISCOMFORT

Up to this point, this book has emphasized creating comfort in colleagues. We have discussed rewarding people, building their confidence, easing their stress, and expanding their sense of competence. In this chapter, we have focused particularly on reducing the tension and problems associated with conflict. All this is necessary and important, but the reader must not overlook the value of discomfort.

One of the prime responsibilities of leadership is to induce and manage (moderate) discomfort. That is why the leadership role is often so lonely. People and organizations that are perfectly at peace, that have no tension, also tend to be dying organisms. It is stress, a sense of the gap between what ought to be and what is, that induces creativity and growth. It is the urge to alleviate discomfort that propels people to higher plateaus and greater achievement. Sometimes that stress is self-induced, but often it requires the vision of leadership to set goals, pose challenges, and describe new heights to be scaled.

The manager who sets great expectations and then supposes that all, or even most, will embrace them with joy and delight is a naive manager indeed. Growth is not comfortable. Therefore, creative tension is necessary for great achievement. Happiness and peace are personal goals to be lauded. But in organizations, contentment and calm are simply precursors to institutional erosion and decline. Great leaders are not often beloved, but they are respected and appreciated by followers who are made to feel stronger and more capable each day.

This caveat is not posed to undercut anything that has been written thus far. It merely adds the realization that the manager of vibrant organizational cultures orchestrates a subtle interplay between increasing personal confidence and a persistent creative longing to do better.

CONFLICT SCENARIOS

To facilitate your mastery of the concepts contained in this chapter, we have included two additional scenarios and a form on which to analyze them. Following each chart is our analysis. How does it compare with yours?

Now it is your turn to analyze the preceding scenario on the Conflict Analysis Form (table 4.12). After you have completed the form, compare your analysis with ours (tables 4.13 and 4.14). Then use the Conflict Pollutants Assessment (table 4.3) to determine the sources of the conflict. Our view is recorded in table 4.15.

Case Analysis

Two conflicts exist here—the major one between Stan Marx and Tom White and emerging secondary friction between Stan Marx and Marge Wilson. The conflict manager needs to deal with both of these conflicts. In the primary one, the problem lies in boundary penetration/expansion, with Tom's role as the central issue. Stan failed to give ongoing feedback when the issue was small; now it has mushroomed. Involved in this issue of working time is also the larger question of Tom's role

Scenario: The Clockwatcher Files a Grievance

Stan Marx, city manager of Calm City, had just hung up the telephone following his conversation with Mrs. Helman of the Citizens for Youth campaign. Mrs. Helman was trying to enlist his aid in persuading the city council to forbid admission of students under eighteen to Starship, a new video arcade less than two blocks from the neighborhood school. Stan was wrestling with the implications of taking a stand on this issue when his train of thought was broken by his secretary.

"Marge Wilson is on line one. She didn't say what the call is about, but she sounds pretty serious." Marge Wilson was completing her second year as director of personnel, and Stan thought of her as a breath of fresh air in the city. Marge knew what life was like in the trenches. She had been a bright, competent go-getter and was chosen to replace the retiring director of personnel. Since Marge had taken over the position, the entire tone of negotiations had taken on a businesslike atmosphere, and a measure of trust and confidence was building on both sides of the table. All in all, Stan was pleased with the new director and had been meaning to tell her so.

"I wonder what the problem is," he thought to himself as he answered line one.

"Stan, we have a mess on our hands, and I need to talk to you as soon as possible."

"What's the matter?" Stan asked.

"Well, in a nutshell, Tom White has filed a grievance against you and has already obtained a go-ahead from the union rep to go all the way with it!"

"What the heck is this all about?" Stan queried. "Tom is pretty much a pain, but I haven't done anything to him to warrant a grievance."

"Well, he thinks so," she answered. "And I believe he may have a point. I'm sorry I can't pursue it further at this time, but I am already late to an important meeting. Can you come in to see me at 2:30?"

"Sure, I'll be there," he mumbled as he hung up the phone. Stan Marx began to retrace his contacts with Tom White over the last few weeks. Tom was a bright, young community center director who was in his fourth year in the city. He did a competent job and got along reasonably well with his fellow workers. If there was one thing about Tom that bugged Stan Marx, however, it was the attitude Tom seemed to have about his job. To Stan, it seemed that Tom did not act like a professional and sometimes appeared to go out of his way to avoid putting in one minute of time beyond that required by the collective bargaining contract. Sure, Tom always showed up to his assigned duties, but he never arrived more than a minute before check-in time. Already twice this year Tom White had stood up to leave a meeting precisely when the clock hit 5 P.M., even though items still remained on the agenda.

Last week, when Stan was on his way to an outside meeting, he noticed that Tom White was leaving the parking lot about thirty minutes before the end of the day. Stan had not said anything at the time but decided to keep his eyes open. Then, the day before yesterday, looking out of his office window, Stan had again seen Tom leaving about thirty minutes early. Stan had become angry.

"Well," he had thought. "It looks as if Tom has decided to change his old game of 'Clockwatcher' to a new one—'Beat the System.' I'd better nip this in the bud." Stan had prepared a note asking Tom to meet with him the next day. The meeting had proceeded more smoothly than Stan had thought it might, with Tom sitting rather quietly throughout. Stan told Tom about seeing him leave early on at least two occasions within the previous two weeks and said he was preparing a letter of reprimand for his personnel file as well as putting him on notice that another violation of policy could lead to further disciplinary action. Following Stan's ultimatum, Tom simply asked, "Is that all?" Stan had nodded assent, and Tom had left the office.

It was a couple of minutes past 2:30 when Stan entered Marge Wilson's office. "Hello, Stan," she said as he sat down. "Thanks for coming on such short notice. This is a hot issue, and I don't want it to get out of hand. You know we are just getting started with negotiations for next year, and it's important that we don't let a bunch of grievances muddy up the waters at this critical stage."

"What's it all about, anyway?" Stan asked.

"Well, it seems that your Mr. White has filed a formal grievance against you charging unequal application of city policy," she responded.

"I don't know what he's talking about," Stan replied, his voice rising with indignation. "I caught him leaving early at least twice in the past two weeks, and I told him he'd better shape up or he could get into trouble. What's wrong with that?"

"Just a minute, Stan," Marge responded calmly. "We're on the same side, you know. Let's see what he says in his formal grievance report." She turned to the second page of the report, then looked up, asking,

"Stan, do you permit any other employees to leave before the official check-out time?"

"Hell, no!" he shouted, his anger little abated by Marge Wilson's calm manner. "My employees often stay long after the required end of the workday." Stan was beginning to warm up to the issue. He continued, "As a matter of fact, I have one of the hardest-working and most professional staffs in the region. White is the only clockwatcher in the group, and when I lean on him a little, you folks hop on his bandwagon. Do you want me to ring a bell and make them all leave at five o'clock when he does?"

"According to Tom White's grievance, Stan," Marge continued in her calm manner, "you wrote a letter of reprimand for his file and threatened him with further disciplinary action when he left a few minutes early one day. Then he says that last month you gave Mrs. Preston permission to leave at 4 P.M.—that's sixty minutes before check-out time— and you also told Mr. Wright he could leave twenty minutes early last week.

"Stan," she continued, "that appears to be a clear case of unequal application of policy. Are his allegations true?"

"Oh, God," he sighed. "Rose Preston is one of the finest and most professional people I have known. She is always the first one at work each day and usually the last one to leave. A real professional who lives for her job and her city! Twice in the last three weeks she has asked to leave a few minutes early to meet with the doctor at the rest home where she has recently had to place her older sister.

"Old Mr. Wright is the salt of the earth. The one person I can always count on. Mr. Wright is completing his twenty-seventh year as a superior Water Department employee. His thirty-fifth wedding anniversary was last week, and he had ordered a special gift for his wife. He received a phone call that the gift had arrived in Centerville, and he needed to leave a few minutes early to pick it up at the store before closing time.

"Of course I gave permission to both of them to leave a little early. I couldn't deny them that opportunity and disregard the concern and help they have so willingly given over the years to the region and the city. I wouldn't have been able to face the rest of my employees or myself if I hadn't allowed them to go."

"Marge, I thought you understood what it is like in management," Stan continued. "Why does everything that is said and done in an office have to be written in the contract? Pretty soon you won't need managers; all you'll have to do is hire a couple of clerks who can read the contract and enforce it! Whose side are you on, anyway? I'm seeing you in a new light."

responsibilities as a professional manager. Tom and Stan need to establish norms on how Tom is to operate; they also need to engage in role analysis for Tom. Since the problem may well exist for others in the department and since role analysis occurs best in groups, we recommend that a small group of managers with related functions be convened and a RAT done for each of them. This may head off later problems. If Tom refuses to accept the norms or roles required of him, he may need to leave the organization. But it is unfair to him to begin with reprimands before the norms and roles are clear and accepted.

As for the secondary conflict with Marge, this can easily be corrected if it is attended to before it grows. Marge and Stan need to recognize why they need each other and establish norms for working together in situations like this. In the future, Stan should be more careful to catch disagreements while they are small and clarify roles early with employees.

Let us now suggest a second scenario for your consideration. What would you do?

Table 4.13. Conflict Analysis Form

Description
Actors:

Subject of Conflict:

Analysis
Conflict Pollutants:

Kinds of Conflict:

Strategy
General Strategy:

Specific Strategy:

Table 4.14.   Conflict Analysis Form (Calm City)

Description:	
Actors:	Primary—Tom White versus Stan Marx
	Secondary—Stan Marx versus Marge Wilson
Subject of Conflict:	Primary—Inconsistent application of policy; professional roles
	Secondary—Marge's allegiance and role
Analysis	
Conflict Pollutants:	Poor feedback
	Mushroom syndrome
	Time
Kinds of Conflict:	Primary—Boundary penetration/expansion
	Secondary—Interpersonal and boundary
Strategy	
General Strategy:	Primary—Norm-setting and role analysis
	Secondary—Norm-setting and establishing interdependence
Specific Strategy:	1. Tom to meet with Stan to discuss norms of operation; involve Tom
	2. Have group of managers meet and do RAT; include Tom
	3. If Tom doesn't agree with role of norms, begin documentation for separation
	4. Have Stan meet with Marge and discuss their expectations for operation in a similar conflict situation; emphasize their interdependence

Table 4.15.   Conflict Pollutants Assessment (Calm City)

In this conflict situation, the following factors are affecting the conflict:

	Not at all	Somewhat			To a great degree
1. Preferences above principles	1	**2**	3	4	5
2. Undue expectations	1	2	**3**	4	5
3. Poor feedback skills	1	2	3	**4**	5
4. Negativism/joylessness	1	**2**	3	4	5
5. Conflict traps					
a. Health	**1**	2	3	4	5
b. Money	1	**2**	3	4	5
c. Time	1	2	3	**4**	5
d. Clutter	**1**	2	3	4	5
6. Mushroom syndrome	1	2	3	4	**5**
7. Poor problem ownership	1	2	**3**	4	5
8. Premature solution	1	**2**	3	4	5
9. "Last tags" complex	1	**2**	3	4	5

Selected values in bold

Scenario: The New Vice President

Bill Turner had been on campus for only a month. He was eager to demonstrate that he was a true leader and innovator. He had been dean of the faculty at a small Midwestern college, where he had been frustrated by the slow pace of change. Now, as academic vice president for Elite University, he hoped to really make things happen. He was eager to shape this university into a great academic institution and saw his first speech before the Academic Senate as a major step in this direction.

After the usual greetings and affirmations, Bill moved to the heart of his ideas. "This university can only reach that vision of greatness through your commitment and hard work. My five-point plan for you, the faculty, is as follows:

1. Each faculty member must publish at least two articles each year.
2. Each faculty member is to establish a growth contract. Department chairs are to be accountable to ensure that faculty members achieve that growth.
3. Within the year, faculty in each department are to examine their curricula and propose ways in which their programs can be changed to excite students and educate them more *effectively*. Departments making the best proposals will be awarded $5,000 in discretionary funds.
4. The Admissions Office will immediately initiate Project Quality, a concerted effort to recruit a more gifted student body.
5. Finally, the university will initiate a major fund-raising effort to support faculty development and services."

After a few closing remarks, Bill waited for reaction. No one asked a question. It was time to sit down and let the faculty take the initiative. He turned to Jim Jeffries and asked, "What is your reaction to this, Jim?"

Jim paused and, with some caution, began "I'm not sure whether I speak for the rest of the faculty, but frankly, I'm offended by your proposal. It seems more like administrative fiat than a collegial message."

Applause broke out in the audience, to which Bill quickly responded, "Please, this is not a game show but an academic forum. Let's keep ourselves to polite interchange." Turning to Jim, Bill then said, "I'm sorry I came across that way, but I'm trying to move our college into the upper elite of academic institutions. For that, strong leadership is needed. I believe that is why you hired me."

Bill then recognized John Wong. "A great university is one that gives faculty freedom and support. Perhaps at Midwest College the faculty needed direction; here we don't. My department trusts what I'm doing, and that is enough. You've been a faculty member; I thought you would be sensitive to that. I've taught math here for twenty-two years and always received great student support. I'm not about to change to become something else. I'm sorry, but don't confuse your needs with those of the university."

Applause broke out once again. Bill looked out at the faculty—some concerned, some laughing, and some leaving.

What should Bill say next?

Analyze the preceding scenario on the Conflict Analysis Form. After you have completed the form, compare your analysis with ours (table 4.16). Then use the Conflict Pollutants Assessment (table 4.3) to determine the sources of the conflict. Our view is recorded in table 4.17.

Case Analysis

The new vice president misread his audience. He prematurely proposed a solution to a problem in which the faculty had no investment or understanding. He would have done better to involve the faculty at an earlier stage. He sounded arrogant and self-righteous; his tone clogged his message.

Clearly, the faculty felt that Dr. Turner had overstepped his bounds and entered into their prerogatives. Probably a value conflict lies hidden here—a value conflict about the fundamental purpose of a university—but more information is needed to confirm this. The faculty may see the university as a musty, unchanging place; Turner wants it to be an "elite" institution.

To find a way out of this conflict, Turner must first retreat from his five-point plan. The faculty is not ready, and he will only meet failure if he tries to push it. Instead, he should emphasize the importance of

Table 4.16.   Conflict Analysis Form (Elite University)

Description:	
Actors:	Bill Turner versus the faculty
Subject of Conflict:	Turner's five-point plan for the faculty
Analysis	
Conflict Pollutants:	Undue expectations
	Feedback skills
	Premature solution
Kinds of Conflict:	Boundary penetration
	Values
Strategy	
General Strategy:	Norm-setting
	Interdependence
	Problem-solving
Specific Strategy:	1. Retreat from five-point plan
	2. Emphasize mutual need
	3. Convert from value conflict to tangible conflict by using problem-solving
	4. Establish norms for role of the vice president

Table 4.17.   Conflict Pollutants Assessment (Elite University)

In this conflict situation, the following factors are affecting the conflict:

	Not at all		Somewhat		To a great degree
1. Preferences above principles	1	**2**	3	4	5
2. Undue expectations	1	2	3	4	**5**
3. Poor feedback skills	1	2	3	4	**5**
4. Negativism/joylessness	1	**2**	3	4	5
5. Conflict traps					
a. Health	**1**	2	3	4	5
b. Money	**1**	2	3	4	5
c. Time	**1**	2	3	4	5
d. Clutter	**1**	2	3	4	5
6. Mushroom syndrome	**1**	2	3	4	5
7. Poor problem ownership	**1**	2	3	4	5
8. Premature solution	**1**	2	3	**4**	5
9. "Last tags" complex	**1**	2	3	4	5

Selected values in bold

the faculty and his interest in working with them. He should then create a faculty task force to consider his plan and propose one of its own. This will move the conflict to the tangible level—how will we use our resources to accomplish certain ends? He also needs to meet with key institutional leaders and clarify the informal norms by which he should operate. He obviously violated them.

CHAPTER 5

Dealing with Difficult People

The previous chapter on managing conflict examined the conflict pollutants that clog the climate, analyzed the types of conflict in which we find ourselves, described the strategies that resolve conflict, and matched the strategies to the conflict types. But what happens when you run into people who do not respond to such rational attempts at conflict resolution? These people always want to be in conflict. They are difficult people. Difficult people come in thirteen types. The following real-life scenarios will introduce you to them. After you have seen the full range of difficult folks, we will tell you how to deal with them.

THE TYPES

Irrational Type

The board meeting of the Peacock Valley School had come to the public forum section of the agenda, but before the president could call for the first speaker, a man in the back of the room moved forward rapidly, yelling, "How can you even think of allowing sex education in our schools? Schools are for academic pursuits! You have no right teaching my child about sex! I won't allow you to teach sex in the schools."

The president pounded her gavel and interjected, "Excuse me, but we spent several months looking at all aspects of sex education. We had a parent/teacher committee that met regularly. . . ."

The man cut her off, his voice rising, "I don't want sex education in our schools. Sex education shouldn't be in schools. I don't want it! I don't want it!!"

With the irrational type, the problem is not the content of the issue but the inability of the person to hear anyone else. This type is impervious to communication.

The Recognition Seeker

The management team of the Personnel Division had been meeting for about half an hour when Joe Starlet burst into the room!

"Sorry I'm late again, the traffic was lousy, and just as I went to pull into a place in the parking lot, someone beat me to it! What have I missed?"

The team leader asked Joe to sit down and take a few minutes to get caught up.

Moving noisily to his chair, Joe dropped his notes as he spoke up. "But I need to know what you've discussed. I have ideas about many of the items on the agenda, so if someone would just do a recap for me, I'd appreciate it."

Arriving late happens to all of us at some time, but for a few people, this is a life pattern representing not the lateness itself but a need for attention and notice. Late arrival is but one manifestation. Other examples include the professional resister and the organizational cynic, both of whom have unconditionally negative responses to change.

The Bully

Mr. Smith came barging into the office of Ms. Sweet, the school principal. "I want my child taken out of Mrs. Moore's class immediately!" he shouted as he leaned over the desk. "That teacher is not right for my son! I want you to change him today, before I leave your office!"

Ms. Sweet responded, "Mr. Smith, your son is placed where he belongs."

"Are you telling me I don't know what is good for my son? I don't care what you say! If you don't change him, I'm calling the superintendent. Then we'll see what happens!"

The bully loves confrontation. He wins by intimidation and focuses on the battle at hand.

He has little long-range perspective.

Space Cadet

Mrs. Adams had made an appointment with the principal to discuss her first-grade daughter's class placement. Mrs. Adams began the conference by saying sweetly, although she was obviously disturbed, "I really want my child changed to Mrs. David's class because she does marshmallow art with her class and my little Sally didn't get to do that with her teacher, Mrs. Zeal. All of Sally's friends got to do the marshmallow art but she didn't."

The principal tried to calm her, "But Mrs. Adams, Mrs. Zeal is a mentor teacher. She offers the students many wonderful art experiences, computer activities, and many other interesting lessons."

Breathlessly Mrs. Adams went on, "But she doesn't do marshmallow art. Sally wants to have some marshmallow art hanging on the refrigerator just like her friend Mary. Sally is so upset and the marshmallow art is so creative and fun for the kids."

While this scenario may seem implausible, it is a true incident! The space cadet is in a different world. Whatever you say fails to touch his or her reality.

Hidden-Agenda Type

Two colleagues, Steve and David, had been working diligently on researching and preparing a joint project presentation for the president of Savmor Insurance Company. Today they were meeting to complete their plans and develop the presentation. Unbeknown to Steve, David was up for possible promotion, and this presentation would have a big impact on the decision.

Steve arrived with completed presentation boards, overhead transparencies, and notes in hand. David entered and was taken aback at seeing everything already in finished form.

"Well, what do you think?" asked Steve beaming.

David replied tentatively, "Fine, the presentation boards look fine. But I don't like the transparencies."

Steve asked incredulously, "What's the matter with the transparencies? They depict everything we've researched."

David replied, "I think they could be different, more self-explanatory. Maybe they need a little more color. Yeah, I think I have some ideas on how they could be changed for the better."

Once again, all of us will have hidden agendas at times, but some people repeatedly hide their intents and needs. Very often they embroil us in fights over the secret, not the real, agenda.

Oblivious Type

Pam is out on the golf course ready to tee off when Frank approaches, talking as he comes. "You've got a great swing. Did you take lessons or is it natural?"

Pam turns around and gives him "the look" to caution him to be quiet and prepares once again to tee off

"Oh, sorry, go ahead and hit the ball," Frank apologizes.

Once again Pam goes into her swing . . .

"I wish I had a natural swing. Try as I might I feel so clumsy!" babbles Frank as he paces a yard away.

"Do you mind?" asks Pam.

"Oh, there I go again," he sighs apologetically once more. "Don't mind me—go ahead and hit. It is your turn, after all."

Pam gets in a practice swing to put her mind back in the game. Just as she steps up to swing again. . .

"Great swing, do you think you can teach me how to do that?"

The oblivious type is impervious to feedback. These people do not mean harm, but they repeatedly violate the needs of others. They simply do not realize what they are doing.

Whiner

The director has been waiting expectantly for the project report Jan Jones is to deliver today. Suddenly, Jan arrives sans report.

"Where is the report?" asks the director.

"I couldn't get the report finished," she says. "I didn't have enough time. Can you give me more time? I know I can get it finished if you just give me two more weeks," she begs.

"But you've had a month," replies the director.

"I know, but I've had so much to do and two other projects had to be finished during the same time," she complains with a whine.

"Didn't you accept this time frame when you were given the project?" the director asks rationally.

Jan pleads, "But I didn't know how hard it would be or how much time it would take. Pleeeassse, give me more time. Pleeeassse!"

The whiner wears you down through tone. A whiner plays the victim and refuses to accept responsibility for anything.

High-Ground Fighter

The City Council of Middletown was meeting to determine an amount to offer Mr. Yomagura for a strip of his strawberry field that the city wanted to annex. Mr. Yomagura rose to speak.

"You want to take my land away from me without my permission," he said solemnly.

"Mr. Yomagura," the mayor pro tem began, "We do not want to take away your land. We are offering you full market value for the strip we want."

"They took my father's land, too, and sent him to live in a camp during the war. Now you want to take my land as well."

"Mr. Yomagura," the mayor pro tem tried to reason, "We want to pay you for your land."

"I wanted this land to hand down to my son," Mr. Yomagura went on painfully. "Now you are taking it away from me. What will I tell my son when he asks what happened to our land?"

The high-ground fighter fights from a morally or publicly superior position. These contenders have sympathy and public relations on their side.

Wonderfully Nice Person

Principal Maria Garcia wasn't sure what occasion had led to the box of candy on her desk from Mrs. Kim Woods, a second-grade teacher. Later in the day Kim approached her.

"Did you get the candy?" she questioned without waiting for a reply. "You are such a great principal and I appreciate everything you do for me."

Slightly embarrassed, Maria responded, "Thank you, Kim, I appreciate your thinking of me."

Kim continued sweetly, "You always encourage us to try new things, and we all think that is so wonderful. Well, I would like to have some extra funds to buy some animals for my classroom."

"I'm sorry," the principal interrupted. "I have no money for animals for your classroom. The budget has all been spent."

Kim persisted: "The last time I came for extra supplies you were so gracious and found the money. You are such a super principal. I love working for you. I wouldn't want to work with anyone else after working for you. Please, can I have just a little money for the kids?"

When we think of difficult people, we think of nasty types. The wonderfully nice person can also be difficult. These people overpower you with their niceness—and your guilt. You say "yes"—and hate yourself later. You say "no"—and hate yourself immediately.

The Sniper (aka Parking-Lot Contender)

The manager of the service department called in Sam Weston, a service employee known for his grumbling.

"So, Sam, I hear you are unhappy about the decision we all made at the last meeting to work a four-day week," said the manager.

"Who says I'm unhappy?" Sam shot back.

"That's not the point, Sam. The point is that we all agreed to try a four-day week. Now I hear that you are not supporting the decision we all agreed to."

"I want to know the names of the people who say I'm not supportive. Who are they? What did they say?" Sam asked belligerently.

"That's not the point, Sam. Did you try to undercut our decision?"

"No, not me!"

Snipers like to hide behind rocks and trees and cars. They will not confront you to your face, only behind your back. They also seem quite comfortable lying to you.

The Know-It-All

Kevin Barnes had been assigned the task of purchasing new furniture for the offices and waiting rooms at Center City Hospital. He had worked diligently on the task for several months, locating the best commercial furniture at the best price. The purchase list was finally ready to take to the Board of Directors for approval, and Kevin was confident of his selections. The day of the board meeting arrived. The directors had been given the list prior to the meeting.

"Mr. Barnes," began Mrs. Coulten, "I see you have put together quite an extensive list for us to approve."

"Yes," replied Mr. Barnes with pride. "I spent a great deal of time researching and comparing before compiling the list."

"Well, what I don't understand then, Mr. Barnes, is how you could even suggest that we pay these prices for tables and chairs! I have been doing some shopping of late myself for my home and I can get much better prices than the ones you have quoted here. Furthermore, I don't think we need to have this fancy fabric. Why, in my house, plain is good enough for my family. I think I could have found much better prices."

Mr. Barnes started to respond, "Mrs. Coulten, I appreciate your comments, but I really did look into each and every item . . ."

He got no further as Mrs. Coulten continued. "Mr. Barnes, I will be glad to give you a list of the places I have been shopping and you will see I can get much better prices."

The know-it-all knows everything about everything. These difficult people have read, seen, tried, and experienced it all. They *are* superior, if we can judge from their tone and attitude.

Passive Resister

The staff of Westmont Middle School had been involved in a heated discussion on the direction of after-school activities. Some members were anxious to move away from competition and toward activities that would include all students. Cindy Steward had been lounging in the back of the room, not participating in the discussion. Finally, someone suggested that a trial run was possible. They were trying to reach consensus on opening up all activities to all interested students for one semester to see how it would go over.

The facilitator asked Cindy how she felt.

"Go ahead and do whatever you want to do. You always do anyway," Cindy replied disinterestedly.

"But Cindy, we really want to know how you feel," urged the facilitator.

"Do whatever you want; you never listen to me anyway!" Cindy insisted.

The passive resister does not like to be direct but likes to control through guilt and last-minute comments. Passive resisters share indirection with the sniper. They control best in group settings.

The Indecisive

The superintendent of Eagle School District, Dr. John Lathrop, was engaged in discussion with a member of the school board, Mr. Biff Brown. The school board would shortly be deciding budget cuts to make for the next year.

Dr. Lathrop began by sharing the many recommendations developed by staff. "We have academic, athletic, extracurricular, transportation, and maintenance programs to review, as you can see from this long list. Which of these programs would you favor cutting?"

Mr. Brown responded, confused, "I don't know. What do the others think?"

"I think it is going to be important for each of you to decide and then work collectively," the superintendent answered.

"I need more data. Can you get me more information on each of these?"

Exasperated, the superintendent replied, "We've given you all the data over the last three months."

In a clearly indecisive tone, Mr. Brown said, "Oh, that's right. Which one do you favor? And maybe we need more time before deciding."

Indecisives never seem to reach a decision. More data, more time, more options—these are the constant complaints. Put under pressure, indecisives want someone else to choose for them.

THE RESPONSES

Now that you have been introduced to the thirteen types of difficult people, how many have you recognized? Is it fair to ask whether you ever fall into these patterns? We often ask clients to bring a difficult person to mind as we discuss general and specific responses to their behavior. Before reading on, try to think of particular individuals you know who fit these types. Think about how you have been handling them.

General Responses

First, let's take a look at the general responses that work with all thirteen types of difficult people. Table 5.1 lists them for you. The gen-

Table 5.1.   General Responses to Difficult People

1. Don't try to change a difficult person
2. Diagnose difficult type(s)
3. Stay calm and self-assured
   - Maintain leverage
4. Control the process
   - Try the out-of-body tactic
   - Be strategic
5. Be patient
   - Choose your time
   - Choose your issue
6. Set norms
7. Search for a win
   - Give people a way out
   - Value them
8. Use body language
9. Remember that a difficult person speaks only for the difficult person

eral responses should become an automatic part of your management repertoire. These responses will keep you in control of conflictual situations, allowing you to be proactive in situations even though the difficult person prefers to put you in a reactive mode.

Don't Try to Change a Difficult Person

Difficult people have been years in the making. You cannot hope single-handedly to make great strides in improving their behavior. If you focus on the issue and how to deal with the type, you will find yourself farther ahead. Changing a difficult person is not possible in a work environment. Limit yourself, therefore, to altering your behavior and theirs so that you will be able to work together. Peaceful, if only partially peaceful, coexistence should be your goal.

Diagnose Difficult Type(s)

Since appropriate responses vary with the types, it is critical to place the difficult person in one of the categories just described. As you will see later, selecting a response that is *in*appropriate may inadvertently give the person power or recognition, thus causing him or her to become more difficult.

Stay Calm and Self-Assured

Nothing throws a difficult type more than to have an adversary who maintains leverage by remaining calm and self-assured. Keep in mind that one of the biggest difficulties with difficult people is *yourself.* You get frustrated and angry and lose your poise. When that happens, the difficult person wins.

Control the Process

An out-of-body experience is often necessary. What do we mean by that? Pretend you are a third-party observer to the situation. Do not let yourself listen to the whine or the sweetness of the Wonderfully Nice Person. Instead, focus on the content of the plea. Evaluate the arguments from a neutral position, as if you had no investment in the situation but were standing on the outside looking in.

Appreciate the difficult person's strategies. In the heat of the conflict, look at the person and say to yourself, "That was an effective bully tactic" or "great whine" or "nice oblique shot." In this way, you keep your sense of humor and your control.

Another way to control the process is to be strategic. Allowing the difficult person to withdraw from the current situation often calms the situation. Perhaps, as with the next strategy, you might schedule further discussion at a different time. Teach yourself the habit of thinking strategically. Do not be engulfed by the passion of the moment and make the mistake of jumping in immediately.

Be Patient

As you can see from the scenarios presented, you will not find it easy to be patient with the difficult person. Nevertheless, patience is an essential strategy because, faced with it, the difficult person often wears out. Should that happen, you have the opportunity to step in with one of the specific responses outlined in the following pages. If the issue raised by the difficult individual does not require immediate response, then control the timing yourself. Schedule an appointment at your convenience so you can maintain leverage in the situation.

Set Norms

Be assertive in setting ground rules for discussing the issue. Make sure the difficult person realizes that every person involved will get air time. Establish a norm to the effect that all sides of the discussion will be considered. Norm-setting takes but a little time and turns attention away from the issue for a brief moment. This focus on procedures gives breathing room, if only momentarily.

Search for a Win

Difficult people need to feel that their requirements are being met. A smart manager looks for a win-win solution. Somewhere in all that is said, search for a clue to a way to make the difficult person feel like a winner. Be open to that solution.

Use Body Language

Use your eyes. Give the difficult type "the look." But use body language appropriately. The Wonderfully Nice Person will become quiet under "the look," but the Space Cadet and the Oblivious Type will not even notice.

Use your hands. If the difficult person is the Recognition Seeker, talking out of turn, hold up your hand like a stop sign in her face as you ask her to wait. Body language sends clear messages to some difficult types.

Remember, a Difficult Person Speaks Only for the Difficult Person

An oft-used ploy of the difficult person is to claim, "Well, others think as I do." Do not fall into this trap. Take the difficult types as entities in and of themselves. Rarely are others standing behind them. Deal with each type individually—and appropriately.

Specific Responses

Each of the thirteen types of difficult people has its own responses. The specific responses for each of the types, summarized in table

5.2, give managers a range of strategies for dealing with difficult people.

The Irrational Type

. . . is best handled by letting them talk. By expending energy, the Irrational Type will eventually run out of things to say. If you have been a good listener, you have discovered a few key words that summarize what the Irrational Type is after. Ask questions using those key words. Questions tend to calm people down. Once the Irrational Type becomes engaged with your questions, you can turn the discussion in the direction you want.

The Recognition Seeker

. . . is accustomed to getting negative behavior. This type will do virtually anything to get someone to notice them. To counteract the Recognition Seeker, you must withdraw recognition for negative behavior while simultaneously targeting positive behavior with praise. Bring Recognition Seekers on the inside of things. Involve them. Empower them with information.

The Bully

. . . is trying to overpower you. Do not retreat! Once you do, the Bully will be back, ever stronger and more insistent. Keep calm. Do not allow yourself to become overpowered by the threats that will no doubt come your way. This is a perfect type on which to practice the out-of-body tactic. Try to stand back to hear what the Bully wants. And remember you are in this for the war, not the small skirmishes. An excellent strategy to use with a Bully is to move the discussion side by side. Sit next to the Bully. Ask the Bully to walk with you as you check on an emergency. Nothing derails a Bully faster than not being able to "get in your face."

Table 5.2. Specific Responses to Difficult People

Irrational Type	• Let energy be spent • Ask questions • Find key word • Give direction
Recognition Seeker	• Bring inside • Give praise • Withdraw recognition for negative behavior
Bully	• Stay calm (out-of-body tactic) • Stay strong; don't retreat • Don't worry about battles; go for the war • Use side-by-side strategy
Space Cadet	• Agree and go on • Use their words to restate your point
Hidden-Agenda Type	• Explore agenda • Ask questions • Avoid guilt
Oblivious Type	• Direct feedback • Replicate behavior • Create unease • Face to face
Whiner	• Cut off their tone (out-of-body tactic) • Accept message
High-Ground Fighter	• Retreat
Wonderfully Nice Person	• Stick to your agenda • Avoid guilt (out-of-body tactic) • Know what *you* want
Sniper	• Bring into the open • Establish public norms
Know-It-All	• Test knowledge • Listen • Harness them • Give tasks incrementally • Focus on content, not style
Passive Resister	• Involve • Draw out in public • Avoid guilt if passivity continues
Indecisive Type	• Ask many questions • Be careful of problem ownership • Avoid guilt

The Space Cadet

. . . can go on forever over nothing. It is best just to agree and go on. Use *their* words to restate *your* position so they feel their concerns are being addressed. Do not waste a lot of time with the Space Cadet.

The Hidden-Agenda Type

. . . is after just one thing—and most of the time you do not even know what the thing is. Explore that secret agenda by asking clarifying questions. In our scenario, David wanted to be able to show off for the boss, but he did not want to come straight out and say so. Steve should keep asking questions of David. How would David do it differently? What does he not like? . . . and so forth. Steve might even ask if there was something bothering David. In dealing with Hidden-Agenda Types, be careful not to lose your agenda to theirs. And do not feel guilty about moving on with the initial agenda.

The Oblivious Type

. . . needs to be confronted head on. Frank was bound and determined to interrupt Pam on the tee. Only when Pam takes command, tells Frank straightaway that he is to stop talking during play, and then actually replicates the talking when Frank is ready to tee off will Frank get the message. If the Oblivious Type is not uncomfortable to the point of feeling unease, the difficult behavior will continue.

The Whiner

. . . has had years to practice and perfect that whine. You will never correct it. The Whiner calls for the out-of-body tactic. Say to yourself, "What a great whine! On a scale of one to ten, it is worth at least an eight." Try then to accept the message underneath the whine. In our scenario, the director must get past the begging and pleading to determine if there truly *was* insufficient time to complete the project and then either reestablish a reasonable time line or assign the task to a more qualified employee.

The High-Ground Fighter

. . . has you. Retreat as fast as you can and begin to think strategically about the issue. Mr. Yomagura is definitely a High-Ground Fighter. Who could argue with him and win? Down the road, though, he would probably need to win over a majority on the City Council. Perhaps he had already reached that level and just did not realize it. The mayor pro tem had no choice but to back off and either think of another way to get the needed land or drop the issue altogether. He may be on the right side of the moral issue. That is not the problem. Instead it is the strategy he is using.

The Wonderfully Nice Person

. . . gets you with guilt! Refuse to give in to it. In our scenario, the principal had already capitulated once before, a fact the Wonderfully Nice Person reminded her of forcefully. Do these difficult people go away? No, they come back at you again and again. Your recipe for dealing with the Wonderfully Nice Person? Stick to what you think is important, know what you want, and do not deviate from it.

The Sniper

. . . is also known as the Parking-Lot Contender because the parking lot is where most of this type's discussions take place. On the surface, Snipers support you and the decisions made by the group, but behind your back—look out! You have only one option with the Sniper, and that is to bring him or her out in the open. Agreed-upon norms provide the accountability factor you want to have in place with Snipers. Be direct and confront!

The Know-It-All

. . . has a better way, can do it better, and can offer more suggestions than anyone else, especially after the fact. It is important to test the knowledge base of this type. The Know-it-All may actually be an expert. By focusing on the content of what a Know-It-All says, not the style that is used to convey the message, you may find some real expertise. Test that knowledge by giving the Know-It-All small expert tasks to complete. In this way, you are harnessing energy that would otherwise be used for "you should have asked me."

The Passive Resister

. . . is the supreme difficult person. This type builds a reputation on his or her consistently negative behavior and refusal to participate. As a result, the Passive Resister becomes the center of attention whenever he or she is asked to be involved. The Passive Resister needs to be brought into the discussion, given an opportunity to respond, and asked to declare or refuse to support a group consensus. By bringing the Passive Resister out into public awareness, you let everyone experience the responses. If the Passive Resister continues to be so, then you must avoid guilt. He or she has had the opportunity to participate and refused. Let the Passive Resister know that the group is moving ahead, with or without his or her input.

The Indecisive

. . . can't make a decision. Indecisives always want more information or more input or more time. They hate accountability; they simply cannot choose among a variety of alternatives. To work with the Indecisive, you should only offer binary choices—either/or, yes/no, alternative A or B, and the like. An effective manager provides the Indecisive with just two choices at a time, then compels him or her to make the choice. Most of the difficult types will try to shift the problem to you. Do not let them do so—the problem is theirs and they must solve it. Moreover, do not allow yourself to feel guilty or uneasy about their indecision— that will only lead you to make the decision for them. Provide binary choices and stick to them!

Teachers

A particular subset of difficult people—teachers—was explored by Hixson (1997). She found the exact array of difficult types and strategies to deal with them as we have found. She found the bully, passive, irrational type, the sniper, and know-it-all to be must pervasive. She also found that administrators tended not be very diverse in their coping strategies. Just as we pointed out—the better you are in using the right strategy for the right type of difficult person, the more successful you'll be.

CONCLUDING NOTE

There are many subcategories for the basic types of difficult person: Petulant Child, Negative High Priestess, Sponger, Arrogant Wonder, and so forth. The list could go on. Our purpose has been to acquaint you with the thirteen broad categories we have identified. Our premise remains that conflict resolution comes about when conflict is managed—and managed correctly. At the base of all conflict resolution is analysis. Analyzing what you are dealing with gives you control and provides you with energy to deal with the conflict and move forward in implementing the plans and realizing the goals of the organization.

As we said at the beginning of this chapter, conflict is a different kind of building block than the others that preceded it. Nevertheless, its role is central to building positive environments.

Conflicts will occur. Conflicts should occur. When managers understand how to use conflicts to advance organizational goals and enrich people interaction, they know a key building block of strong organizations.

CHAPTER 6

Teams and Politics

More and more team-building is necessarily involved with external politics. This came to me first in 1984 when I was first elected as a city council member. I came on to a city council that was split down the middle. I was to be the deciding vote, but I did not want to be. I wanted a team discussion. So I went about crafting a team. To do so, I had to forge an alliance in the community. I had to deal with external politics. I never forgot that lesson—team-building for many public administrators must deal with politics. For with politics come issues of power.

Pfieffer (1981) argues that power, or politics, enters an organization if three things are present:

1. Scarcity of resources
2. Conflict over priorities
3. Ambiguity over goals

For most of us, not one, but three, are present—we can't help dealing with politics. In a neat world of rationality, it would not be necessary to cope with power, but we are not in such a world. We have to deal in politics whether we like to or not, and, for the most part, we do not like it. But that attitude is irrelevant. We have to manage politics if we want to build strong teams.

STRATEGIES

At least nine strategies are associated with managing politics. They are meant as a recipe for survival, as a means to the end of a harmonious organization.

Catch Things When They Are Small

Leaders can ignore an issue when it is small, but it will soon mushroom out of control. A board can ignore a request for a $1,000,000 purchase but bitterly contest a $100 conference fee. Nothing is small in politics. You must treat each case as if it were big and manage it appropriately.

Remember That All Politics Are Local

Do not think that politics is merely the domain of the state or federal government. It is local. People most care about, and have the most conflict over, the streets, public safety, schools, their jobs, Little League, churches, and the like. National defense is important, but they don't care. Domestic policies are what affect people's lives, and they are comprised of mostly local issues. So if you manage your local affairs, your town council, your school board, your local community, your parents, you'll handle 95 percent of the politics that you will be required to manage.

Build Trust

This is the most important of all the prescriptions (Gibb 1961). You build trust with your staff and your staff teachers; you build trust with your community; you build trust with your central office. You build trust with everyone. By building trust, we were able to pass a utility tax by a majority of 79 percent when others were going down to defeat. With trust built, one district was able to pass a bond issue by 75 percent when outsiders said it couldn't be done and when other tax measures were going down in defeat.

Trust isn't an action itself; it is a result of other actions. These other actions are:

1. *Interdependence.* When both parties say out loud what they need—you need me, and I need you. When one doesn't need the other, or perceive it to be such, he can act in an arbitrary and capricious manner. When we act cooperatively we can establish trust.

2. *Consistency*. There is consistency from word to word and word to deed. When you say the same thing to one person that you say to another, that is consistency. When you do what you say you'll do, that is consistency. If you say different things to different people or do not do what you say you'll do, you will violate trust.
3. *Honesty*. You tell the truth, such as when a board opens up its books during negotiations or administrators give honest feedback to teachers.
4. *Affability*. You are a likable person. It is hard to trust someone who is a pain in the neck. There is a reason this item is fourth on the list—the others are more important, but it does play a part.

These are the attitudes that build trust; without them you have no trust at all. With them you have the opportunity to achieve much. But remember that for every ounce of energy you invest in sowing distrust, it takes five ounces of energy to sow trust.

Don't Wait to Build Networks Until You Need Them

Build networks well ahead of time. Get to know people, whether they be school parents, botanical garden boosters, cub scouts, senior citizens, Chamber of Commerce members, mobile home residents, Pop Warner Football, or the like. You do things for their group. Help them. Go to everything. Then when you need them, they will be there to help you. If you wait until you need them, then go to meet them, they will see your actions as manipulative. If you wait to go to senior citizens until you need to vote a bond issue, you have waited too long. Build networks ahead of time.

Build Coalitions

Start with assessing your community. Do a community scan:

'

* Assess the key groups in the community
* Assess the leaders of the community
* Assess the "take" of community leaders on important issues

- Assess the demographics in the community
- Assess the issues they would like to see something done about

Once you've done a community scan, you are ready to form a coalition—whether it be for a board issue or child abuse advocacy or football stadium repair or fourth-grade reading. You build a coalition by identifying :

1. An issue
2. A group that can work with you on the issue (then increasing the size of this group)
3. Why the issue is urgent
4. Ways to foster confidence that the task can be completed
5. Ways to reward those who support the issue

Celebrate Everything

You can't have too much celebration. Celebrate the accomplishments of teachers, staff, parents, retirees, administrators, and the like. We once gave out "I did it" stickers at a staff meeting to celebrate the teachers' reading achievements in helping student reading scores improve. Before long every teacher wanted the sticker. When all had eventually earned them, they again celebrated. We sent out thank-you notes praising them for what they had done. In many of the classrooms, the notes were placed on teachers' bulletin boards. They prized them so much. We never hear enough great things said about us. Celebrate everything and the goodwill generated will return many times over.

Include All Sides

In solving problems or planning strategies or building coalitions, don't just include your supporters. Include your resisters also. "Pay me now or pay me later" might be the motto. You have to test out your ideas sooner or later; you might as well do it sooner (Harvey 1990).

By including those opposed to your issue or idea, you have a chance to persuade them. You have a chance to acquaint them with your ideas and concerns so that they might be proponents rather than opponents. You also might alter your ideas. They might make good points.

Including all sides will make the solution strong and more readily acceptable at the end. We remember working on the issue of mobile home rent control. We pledged to find a solution to the thorny problem in our city. When inflation was going up 4 percent, rents were going up 12 percent. We formed a problem-solving group, which included all sides—the owners of the parks and the residents. They had never met before. Through some discussion and persuasion, we came up with a solution and it still stands today, eighteen years later. But the key point is that we included all sides.

What Comes Down and the How Comes Up

The job of leaders is to have a vision. The role of leaders is to say what will happen. To do less is to abrogate leadership. But once that is done, you must have everyone involved in how the decision will be implemented.

Once we were hired by a milk-processing company to see why so many glass containers were being broken. Earlier that year the company had had an engineering firm design a crate for the storage and delivery of the milk bottles. They designed a new crate, but breakage went up. So in talking to men down on the line and plying them with ice cream sundaes, we learned that the men were breaking the bottles. "What right do the 'suits' have to tell us how the crate should look?" they said. So we got agreement from the suits. The men could design the crate after the suits specified the criteria. The men went to work. The crate they came up with wasn't that much different from the one that the engineers had designed. But it was theirs, and breakage went down to about nothing. The suits specified the what; the men specified the how.

Live by Quid Pro Quo

Nobody does anything without a reason. People may do something because it appeals to their sense of fair play. Maybe a certain action earns them a decent reward. Maybe there is a certain logic behind their actions. Maybe they are supporting a friend. Whatever the reasons, people get something out of what they do. If you think that people will support schools simply because you're "good," you're dealing in an unrealistic world. Always ask yourself what's in it for them from their perspective.

CONCLUDING NOTE

If you keep these nine strategies in mind, you'll be able to craft political alliances that will be sure to build better teams.

CHAPTER 7

Endowing People with Power

'

Once upon a time there was a world in which one man could control all the forces around him with the power of his will. That world, whether of fable or reality, is gone. The days of centralizing power in the hands of one person who compels everyone to follow him obediently died long ago, perhaps on the plains of the Mongols . . . or with the rise of modern unions . . . or when legislatures mandated inclusion of minorities and women in the workplace . . . or as a result of the increased educational level of the modern worker. The reasons are myriad. But for many people, the myth of that kind of power remains. They expect to command in a world where that power strategy no longer works. A recent book that invokes nostalgia for that power is *The Leadership Style of Attila the Hun* (Roberts 1987). In attempting to relate the world of the Huns to the 1990s, the author merely confuses what we know about leadership and power by reinforcing the myth of traditional power strategies.

LEADERSHIP AND POWER

David McClelland (1970) offers a fascinating research perspective on this issue of leadership and power. He argues that each of us is driven to leadership by at least one of the following three motives:

- Achievement: the desire to complete tasks and accomplish goals
- Affiliation: the desire to be liked and to share in positive relationships
- Power: the desire to exert influence.

While all of us carry some elements of each, one of these motives predominates in each of us. Which is your dominant motivation for leadership? If you are like most managers, you will choose "achievement." In our work we have found that 70 percent of school and business managers express their motivation in terms of task or goal accomplishment. And therein lies a major dilemma for organizations.

Achievement

Those who are driven by the desire to achieve tend to be perfectionists. By the same token, they experience trouble with delegation. They were excellent followers and task achievers—that is why they were promoted to management. They got things done! Now, as managers themselves, they are disappointed with the achievement of others—it is never as good as their own, never as good as they expect. They respond either by taking back tasks or by failing to delegate them. They do the work themselves, hence becoming more and more overloaded—or they suffer sheer frustration, recurrently pointing out to employees their persistent shortfalls.

Neither response works. Managerial positions now and in the foreseeable future embrace such a wide span of control and such a broad range of requisite tasks that no one can "do it all." Those who try, simply burn themselves out. Alternatively, waiting for shortcomings on the part of others is equally destructive because the leader, in his or her frustration, becomes increasingly unhappy, creating toxicity that seeps through the rest of the organization. High motivation to achieve is a poor basis for leadership. Great in followers, it is poor in managers.

Alas, we have all worked for such leaders. High achievers want great accomplishments, but their tyrannical behavior squelches high-risk thinking in their subordinates. I remember a brilliant researcher and theorist who became dean of education at a major university. I was his assistant, and he was the modern Attila. He expected much of everyone, including himself. He was a perfectionist of the first order. Never knowing what might arouse his ire, I spent each day hoping merely to survive. In his demand for perfection, this man let all of us know our failings. The result was little daring—not even honesty. I lasted one year and left. I achieved neither highly nor long. The motivation to achieve is a weak basis for leadership.

Affiliation

Those with a high need for affiliation also encounter great problems in leadership. They want to be liked and to experience positive relationships. The dilemma is that given limited resources and conflicting demands, certain leadership situations are lose-lose. You will anger someone, no matter what you do or fail to do. Those driven by affiliation will often feel lonely and yearn to be part of the group. They will stress that they rose through the ranks—"I was a teacher too" or "I know what it is like to work on the line." But this approach does not last long. Leadership may engender respect, but it seldom engenders friendship. The only option, if this leader is to succeed, is to meet affiliation needs outside the organizational setting. Otherwise—even in positive, joyful organizations—leaders with high affiliation needs are frequently overcome by the loneliness of their position.

Power

Power is the leadership motivation least often chosen by managers, but it is the most effective. This conclusion is McClelland's greatest contribution. He describes "two faces" of power. The first is the desire for personal dominance—the "king-of-the-hill" motif. In this face of power the rewards come from winning, from beating others out. I hold power close to my chest, and I let you know I have it.

Every child who has faced a schoolyard bully or a social climber is familiar with this type of power. Have you ever attended a high school reunion? Those who felt overwhelmed and overpowered throughout high school return to demonstrate their current power—whether in the form of money, cars, spouse, or image. King-of-the-hill power creates mountains of negative energy and an unending desire to pull the perpetrator off that hill, off that pedestal. Exhilarating but short-lived, it does not work in the long run.

The other face of power is the desire to influence others. This leader finds satisfaction in seeing other people get their jobs done. Your role centers on increasing the competence and capability of others. You recognize that people are imperfect and need support to become more productive. This face of power is the most effective. The term recently

applied to this strategy is "empowerment." This term is more energizing than the word "power," which, probably because it summons up
images of the desire to dominate, carries a negative connotation.

No matter which term you use, recognize that the most effective
approach to leadership focuses on others—emphasizes the growing
competence of everyone in the organization. The fascinating paradox
of power is that, as with love, the more you try to keep it, the more you
lose; the more you give it away, the more you have. People who give
love easily and widely are beloved; people who spread power easily
and widely are powerful. When you make others feel significant and
competent, you will yourself be regarded as significant and competent.
To recall an old saying: "No one is ever as impressed with you as when
you are impressed with them." The messages you send will be the messages you receive.

Given this reality, the best leaders are those who believe in power
and empowerment. We all want to be liked and to achieve goals, but
we do both of these best through empowering others.

> The degree to which the opportunity to use power effectively is granted
> to or withheld from individuals is one operative difference between those
> companies which stagnate and those which innovate. . . . The companies
> with reputations for progressive human-resource practices were signifi-
> cantly higher in long-term profitability and financial growth than their
> counterparts. (Kanter 1983)

A great leader is one who believes in power.

> "Power is the only thing that multiplies when you divide it." (Author
> Unknown)

Sources of Power

If empowerment is indeed the most effective leadership strategy—
and we are convinced it is—then we must understand from whence
power comes. Let us hasten to add that we do not intend to replicate
the literature about power. For that we refer you to Enz (1986), Greiner
and Schein (1988), Kanter (1983), Kaplan (1950), Kipnis (1974),

Kouzes and Posner (1987), Mintzberg (1983), or Pfeffer (1981), to name but a few. Rather, we wish to suggest to you twelve sources of power that operate in most organizations. As you expand the number of people who possess these forms of power, you strengthen the organization. People who have power are

- Needed
- In control of resources
- Flexible in responding to new needs
- Irreplaceable
- Close to decision-makers
- Privy to information
- Able to create consensus and stability
- Interpersonally skilled
- Keepers of institutional memory
- Winners
- Supported by staff
- Professionally credible

Some people have more than one source of power, and the reader could undoubtedly add others, but the important point is that power exists in many different forms. It is not limited to positions of authority. Individuals throughout the organization may exercise significant power; conversely, people at the top of an organization may feel power-*less*. It is the mark of a top-flight organization that many people have power and that different individuals have very different sources of power. The more concentrated and restricted the power sources, the more unstable and toxic the organization.

EMPOWERING PEOPLE

Now let us return to the building blocks for positive organizational climate. To build a strong organization, you start by building strong, powerful people.

Empowerment
is the art of increasing

the competence and capability of others
by endowing them with a sense of self-worth and potency.

But having said this, how do you do it? We suggest eight empowerment principles (table 7.1).

Principle 1. You Empower People When You Give Them Important Work to Do.

Stauffer and Schultz (1988) offer a fascinating image when they describe empowerment as "sharing the chocolate chip cookies." We are all willing to share broccoli or spinach or liver, but chocolate chip cookies are a different matter. We hoard those. When you share the good stuff, the important work, you make others feel important. Conversely, when you share only the uninteresting, tedious jobs, you make others feel useless or demeaned. Tom Sawyer's genius lay in imbuing that fence-painting with a sense of importance. This analogy is not to suggest that you attend only to others' *perceptions* of menial work. You must both elevate the unsatisfying and share the truly satisfying.

For example, think about driving a car. Driving a car is important work in America. Remember the first day you had your driver's license? Remember how important and powerful you felt? That sense of power was not free of anxiety (I drove our Volkswagen through the back of our garage on my first day with a driver's license), but it *was* exhilarating. Remember when your dad let you drive the family somewhere for the first time? Memories of moments of power may last a lifetime. When you give people important work, you allow them to

Table 7.1. Principles of Empowerment

You empower people when you

1. Give them important work to do
2. Grant them discretion in doing their work
3. Give them the resources to do their work
4. Give them praise and recognition
5. Make them feel that their survival is in their own hands
6. Enhance and build task skills
7. Encourage them to work in teams
8. Welcome surprise

become purpose-driven; you promote the passion for achievement. When you demean or disenfranchise people or, withhold important work, they have neither the instinct nor a reason to carry out a purpose. An old adage says:

> Give someone a fish and you feed him for a day.
> Teach someone to fish and you feed him for a lifetime.

When you increase people's skills, when you teach them to do important work, they will do it. Never hoard the chocolate chip cookies; instead, share the important work.

Principle 2. You Empower People When You Grant Them Discretion in Doing Their Work.

Have you ever had someone assign you a reasonably important job and then detail exactly how you are to do it, down to the slightest detail? I remember the first college class I ever taught. I was to teach "the history of academic freedom" to a higher education management class for my advisor, who was going out of town that week. I was excited and decidedly nervous. I did not know whether I could do it, so I retrieved an array of books from the library on the subject. The week before the class, David called me into his office and gave me his notes. He told me just what to say and do. He even provided the appropriate discussion questions. I thanked him . . . and never forgave him. He did not trust me to do well or even to make my own mistakes. I changed graduate advisors the next year, and he never knew why. He later became an academic vice president and then a president with a high need for achievement. To this day, I hear, he is still detailing work for those around him.

When you give important work, also give people discretion to decide how it is to be done. Power exists only with choice. Without choices, I have no capacity to exercise power or to feel significant. Still, an important caveat operates here. When people make choices, they will sometimes make mistakes. The leader with a high need for achievement finds mistakes difficult to withstand; this perfectionist wants success all the time. The empowering leader, by contrast, recognizes that people are imperfect and that his or her job is to help them approach perfection by learning from their own mistakes.

In consulting with many supervisors, we have found three kinds of managers: those who check, those who confirm, and those who trust. Which are you?

The checking manager, unsure of employees' ability to carry out the task, consistently asks for updates and problem-solving sessions to keep the work on target. The checking manager may, in fact, try to take over the task.

The confirming manager selects the best person for the task, gives directions about what is expected, and provides adequate resources. But then, having confirmed that the selected employee is comfortable with the task, this leader allows for questions and offers support when the employee feels the need. The confirming manager steps out of the way to allow the task to be completed, with only intermittent confirmation by the employee that the task is progressing or requires revision.

The trusting manager selects the best person for the task, gives the proper directions and adequate resources, and waits for culmination to occur, trusting in a successful outcome. While each of these styles may be appropriate at one time or another (Hersey and Blanchard 1988), the more you rely on checking or confirming, the less empowerment you have imparted to the organization.

Look back on your own experience. Have you ever sat on the receiving end of tasks delegated by these three types of managers? When did you feel most powerful? Certainly not with the checking manager! Probably you felt most powerful working with the trusting manager. If you are a checking manager and want to modify your style to be more trusting, you must

- Accurately assess the capabilities of each staff member
- Assign tasks based on those strengths and capabilities
- Ensure successful outcomes through a series of small wins

These are the skills that enable managers to grant discretion to others. Certainly it is easier to *say* "give people discretion to do their work" than it is to do so. But its difficulty does not make the principle any less important. Where there is discretion, there is choice. Where there is choice, there is power. Where there is power, one can matter.

Principle 3. You Empower People When You Give Them the Resources to Do Their Work.

Resources exist in many forms. The four traditional categories are

- People
- Money
- Facilities
- Time

If you want people to exercise choice and power, you must provide them with one or more of the above. To do otherwise is like leaving your son the car without gas in the tank. Resources stimulate choices. When you fail to give people adequate resources, you fail to give them power to do their work adequately.

As managers you need to add or expand the fifth resource: *energy*. One problem in this money-scarce era is an increasing reliance on just two resources—time and energy. We call on people to work faster, to put in longer hours, and to do so with greater enthusiasm and creativity than ever before. In so doing, we burn out human resources. Successful organizations know that work must be prioritized and resources directed toward accomplishing that work. This truism is violated in many schools where staffs wrestle with site-based management yet lack sufficient resources to make it work. Teachers are asked to participate in management without the requisite skills or time. A parallel situation occurs in the corporate world, where CEOs continue to call for collaborative strategies but middle managers lack time and understanding to help teams become viable.

Suppose you have insufficient capital to give people more money, equipment, or facilities. What have you done to expand time or to use existing facilities more imaginatively or to create more energy in the organization? Entrepreneurship does not mean simply getting more money. It means actualizing or expanding existing resources—all resources.

Example: As principal of a new school that opened in the middle of the economic recession of the early 90s, I experienced firsthand the power of vision to expand energy. The list of tasks necessary to open school that year seemed unending. Due to severe budget cutbacks, the staff had only three days to ready the school for opening. Books had to be unpacked, materials inventoried, programs planned, students placed, and so forth. Truly, the list *was* endless. The staff, however, was energized by the vision of a new school. We lacked time, money, facilities and people—but energy abounded. A task that was thought to be impossible was completed—with joy and spirit.

Another example: I remember a time the American Youth Soccer Organization (AYSO) approached the city council, wanting fields of their own. They had been relegated to the baseball field and had access to it only as it was available. The city had no money or land to build new fields. In fact, we were trying to eliminate some of our recreational programs to save money. One item on the cut list was kids' T-ball. Although AYSO had people capable of picking up that activity, the reality was that we could not ask AYSO to serve the children of our city without offering the resources to do so. The solution that emerged was far from ingenious, but it worked because it expanded everyone's resources. Starting with the small pool of money we had, we negotiated with the local school district to erect lights on one group of their fields. They would use the fields until 5 P.M.; AYSO, after 5 P.M. The school district gained positive visibility from AYSO parents, Little League had more field space, and AYSO took over the T-ball program. When all was said and done, we had—in effect—expanded space, yet without paying for a single square foot. We actually expanded *time* through shared resources—and everyone ended a winner.

Sharing resources is an important concept for managers to recognize. But let us tell a story that illustrates a caveat. A woman went into a bakery and bought five cookies. The lady at the counter put them into a white bag and then asked if she wished to stay for some espresso coffee. Since that sounded like a good idea, the customer agreed and sat down at the counter to drink her coffee. At one point she searched into the little white bag on the counter and took out one of her cookies. At that moment the man next to her reached into the same bag, pulled out one of the cookies, and smiled at her. She was shocked, taken aback. A little later she retrieved a second cookie from the bag, and the man did likewise. Now she was beside herself. Before she could say anything, he reached in, took out the last cookie, and motioned his intention to split it with her. She was furious. She jumped up, raced out of the bakery, and ran to her car. As she flounced into the car seat, she opened up her purse to find her keys—and saw in her purse the little white bag of cookies she had bought.

There are two morals to this story. The first is that the resources we consider ours may really belong to someone else. We may only be using them. In particular, we do not "own" the resources of our organization; we are only stewards of those resources. Second, sharing graciously may avoid later embarrassment. When we share resources, we expand them for all.

Only a leader driven by passion will succeed in expanding energy. The leader's vision for the organization must be vital, exciting, and clear. To the extent that the vision allows for a united focus and emphasizes an "I can" philosophy, to that extent will it propel workers forward and expand energy. If you want your employees to do important work, give them the resources that matter. Resources fuel choices. And the fifth resource—energy—can compensate for deficits in the other four.

Principle 4. You Empower People When You Give Them Praise and Recognition.

Not all actions deserve praise, but many do. Too often we focus on what is not accomplished rather than what is. As perfectionists and task achievers, we want everything "done right," so we walk around looking to catch people doing something wrong (Blanchard 1982). Praise builds esteem; praise builds people.

One of the great teachers I had was Dr. Ludwig, a professor of American poetry. Every time I offered an interesting insight, he built upon it and waxed enthusiastic. When I was wrong or missed the point, he would muse over my statement and say, "That's one perspective; let's hold that and try another." I knew I had missed the mark, but he told me in a way that let me move forward.

Praise is a powerful and cheap resource, yet we seldom see it. When we do workshops, we often do an exercise called Strength Bombardment in which a group of five to eight people focuses on each member in sequence, recounting for that individual the skills and enrichment each brings to the group. This seems simplistic, but group members exit the exercise aglow. Seldom before have they heard praise. Praise builds that sense of worth and potency necessary to effective practice. When you use praise, remember to

- Do it personally and orally
- Do it in writing
- Do it consistently
- Do it specifically

Praise stickers exemplify this principle. When I began working as a management consultant, I was hesitant about using stickers. I knew they worked with children, but I suspected that adults would discount them. During one early consulting engagement, I was handing out stickers to participants for correct responses as well as active involvement. I wondered how they would react. These were all high-powered managers with a well-known communications company. The participants immediately put the stickers on! At the break, several asked me if I was going to continue handing out the prized stickers, because as yet they had not received one. While some discretion is advised in selecting an appropriate sticker for the group you work with, visual types of praise do work. Stickers can even be designed specifically for your organization to enhance the special recognition. Other forms of visual recognition may also serve.

Principle 5. You Empower People When You Make Them Feel That Their Survival Is in Their Own Hands.

In chapter 1 we described an emerging reality of the 90s—the participative ethic. People want to feel they have control of their own destiny. They want to know that what they do matters. According to classic expectancy theory (Vroom 1964), workers want to know that each X unit of effort gains Y unit of reward. The converse is equally true:

When a worker feels that he cannot affect his rewards no matter what he does, then he has little motivation to achieve.

Many international businesses understand this principle. Restructuring of organizations through participation has been a prominent activity since the 90s. The Japanese have led the way. They empower all employees as part of a team by letting them give input into how their work is accomplished. Deming (1986), with his notion of quality circles, has had a significant, positive impact on Japanese productivity. Scandinavian Airlines established its corporate philosophy on the principle that no matter where one works in the hierarchy of the company, problem-solving is part of the job description. From flight attendants to counter personnel, immediate decisions are made by those who affect the flying clientele. These employees know that the survival of the company and their jobs depend on how well they continuously meet the needs of passengers. Participation brings ownership. Ownership brings hope.

Participation creates a concomitant need for accountability—recognition that every one of us is responsible for what we do. Privilege without accountability becomes license. Both sides of this equation are painfully evident in the raising of children. Children grow and mature as they come to understand that what they do affects their own lives—positively and negatively. Witness the uncontrolled child in the grocery store, or the abused, dispirited child in an institution. The one lacks controls based on accountability; the other despairs of positive consequences. They are equally powerless to build to the future.

The same is true of adults. They must feel that what they do affects their lives—that appropriate rewards and accountability follow from individual actions. Individual discretion and accountability create pride. Many years ago an employee we know placed in the department suggestion box an acronym for a company motto: "P.R.I.D.E. = Personal Responsibility In Daily Effort." Management was impressed and adopted it across the organization. The employee beamed with pride. For several years P.R.I.D.E. was emblazoned on signs and shirts. According to folklore, the employee who suggested it lived up to that motto until the day he retired, a model who inspired others to take on responsibility and to be accountable for their individual actions. P.R.I.D.E. resurfaced just recently—many, many years after its first debut—and the employees still think fondly of its original bearer and the message he spread.

In contrast, if I make sure that you realize that I am your protector and benefactor—that you are nothing without me—I demean your power and diminish your ability to accomplish important things. Self-engendered survival, on the other hand, is an awesome and exhilarating reality. Avis builds its future on that notion, as do many other companies. When I "buy stock" in the future of the organization, I work harder to make it succeed—a simple but significant truth.

Principle 6. You Empower People When You Enhance and Build Task Skills.

One of the great benefits of situational leadership is its focus on task skills (Hersey and Blanchard 1988). One cannot assume that workers have the competence to achieve the work required. When you give people jobs for which they have no skills, you diminish their self-confidence and personal worth. You need to analyze the skill levels of your workers and if they are deficient, build and expand them. As noted earlier, the probability of task deficits is on the rise; through the 90s and beyond the need to educate your employees and expand their task skills will expand dramatically.

Futures experts tell us that most people will change jobs six to seven times in a lifetime. For organizations, both public and private, that means continual change in the workforce. Managers will need to design ongoing opportunities for employees to learn new task skills and refine old ones. This phenomenon of multiple careers will have another dimension—the need to keep trained workers. Training costs can be reduced if an organization succeeds in keeping personnel who have already been trained. Empowered workers tend to support an organization, develop loyalty to it, and remain in its employ. Since it is less expensive in time, money, and energy to enhance job skills of an employee already familiar with the workings of the organization than to train a new hire, this stability—growing out of empowerment—will save training dollars for the organization.

To build these task skills managers must

- Diagnose changing job demands
- Perform a task analysis
- Provide ongoing educational opportunities for all levels of work groups
- Model the skills to be acquired by employees

To diagnose job demands, you need continually to scan the environment and recognize social, technological, and demographic trends. This is a key role of strategic planning. The second function requires an understanding of task analysis—how tasks need to meet changing client and market demands. The third step involves recognition of the increasing educative function of all organizations. The last item deals with the role of modeling skills and behavior. One of the great contributions of Kouzes and Posner (1987) is their emphasis on leadership modeling. As a principal, I enjoyed teaching lessons for new teachers. By modeling the process, I was able to establish which skills I expected while also gaining credibility as an evaluator. The experience provided a common ground for teacher and principal to express concerns and solve problems. All four functions—diagnosis, task analysis, education, and modeling—are essential to building skilled, able employees. All are essential to empowerment.

One company we worked with was a memorable illustration of this principle. The president was a strong and caring leader who did many things right. Nevertheless, her company's market share was declining rapidly. Her service and technology were increasingly outdated. Her company had to change if it was to survive. Recognizing this, she changed all the machines—and her people went crazy. They were out of touch with the new technology. So we were called in. We returned to Step 1. We reanalyzed the environment and examined what she would need—not just in 1990, but in 2000. We then analyzed what her people had to do. With the workers, we designed educational sequences to give them the skills they needed but at a pace they could handle. Finally, we had the president take the same training and use the same technology. Consequently, she understood their fear yet modeled skill achievement. This organization is now highly empowered.

If you believe in empowerment, you also must believe in education.

Task analysis, skill assessment, and education are integral to building effective organizations for the future.

Principle 7. You Empower People When You Encourage Them to Work in Teams.

A fascinating human paradox is that you strengthen individuals when you stress their collegiality with—rather than their isolation from—others. People who feel alone, separate, and self-focused become far more dispirited and selfish than those who feel they are part of a greater whole.

A theme of the current era is the breakdown of traditional mores. The family unit has changed radically from the traditional Mom-and-Dad, Dick-Jane-Spot configuration implanted in our psyches. Whereas this type of family represented 43 percent of U.S. households in 1960, by 1990 that percentage had dropped to 11 percent. A danger in this reconfiguration is that individuals will no longer feel part of a greater whole. Certainly there are many potentially fruitful family types, but each must be driven by a sense of bonding and collective good. We are richer when we are committed to a collective goal.

The same concern surrounds the loss of small town communities. In 1940, 40 percent of Americans lived in towns with a population of less than 40,000; now only 18 percent do so. This loss in what we might call "geographic colleagueship" is another concern for many social demographers, signaling another lost opportunity for focusing on the needs of others, on the collective good.

Perhaps modern replacements for the traditional family unit are emerging. The workplace may be a significant new arena in which to celebrate common goals. People see their work units as "families" or communities. Thus, building teams in organizations may be critical not only to organizational function but also to strengthening individual identity and self-worth. As part of a larger whole, I have greater self-worth, purpose, social responsibility, and hope. Teams enrich individuals while strong individuals also build strong teams.

Principle 8. You Empower People When You Welcome Surprise.

For most managers, surprise is anathema. They love predictability, order, and routine. They hate surprises. But strong, powerful organizations welcome surprise. Harold Enarson, ex-president of Ohio State University, puts it this way:

> There are planners and then there are planners—whether of mountain vacations or of state universities and state systems. There are at least two models: the Cook's tour model and the Lewis and Clark model. The Cook's tour defines a precise schedule on a well-defined route. "If it's Tuesday, this must be Belgium." The tour moves in orderly progression amid known landmarks. The name of the game is to so plan as to avoid contingencies. The unexpected is to be avoided. All is schedule, order, routine.
>
> But I prefer the Lewis and Clark model with its sense of adventure as it explores new frontiers. Lewis and Clark envisioned their goal, assembled the minimum resources, and had the nerve and the courage to take the unexpected in stride. . . . [T]heir epic success was a triumph of small daily successes—all within the context of a goal and a clear sense of direction.
>
> The Cook's tour provides the illusion of planning in a world on imagined stability. The Lewis and Clark tour is an adventure into the unknown. Can there be any choice for us? (Enarson 1975)

While the Lewis and Clark model creates more dread and stress, it also engenders more growth and individual strength. In the Cook's tour model, the individual is a spectator, a passive recipient. While the latter role may be more comfortable, it builds neither individuals nor organizations. Drucker (1985) argues that the opportunity for innovation is greatest at that moment of surprise, at the gap between what has occurred and what was expected to occur. If there is no gap—no surprise—expect no innovation or change. Each of us grows as a result of surprises, whether negative or positive. Some of the surprises we have personally experienced are:

- Loss of job because of funding
- Unexpected pregnancy
- Death of a relative
- Sudden advancement from student to faculty member
- Job transfer
- Election to public office
- Seeing Princeton make the Final Four in basketball.

All of these events, whether major or trivial, have caused individuals to grow. Knowing the growth that follows surprises, astute managers do not attempt to fend off surprise but welcome it and turn it to good use to enrich individuals. This is not an argument for poor planning but rather a recognition that surprises are inevitable and need to become at least useful, if not actually "welcome."

Surprise often brings pain, but at the same time, it provides riches. Have you ever been around someone who was struggling with a problem, pacing around the room, beginning sentences but interrupting himself with "No—that won't work!" Then—suddenly—the head jerks back, eyes light up, fingers begin to snap. "I have it! I have it!" That moment of surprise is magical. As an observer, you become a believer in the idea, whatever it may be, just by watching the process. Watching the light bulb go on, sharing that moment, is electrifying. Teachers experience this phenomenon often. Precisely such surprise responses by students keep many teachers in the profession despite heightened stress.

We worked with one manager who held Build a Better Mousetrap Day once a month. He encouraged all employees to look at the organization and tell him what was not working and what had turned out better than expected. Teams then brainstormed what "mousetrap" would make the organization better. Everything was handled in a mouse motif. For example, cheese was always served. The day was a joyful celebration of surprise, and everyone was strengthened by it. Surprises occur constantly. When you capitalize on them, you build individual strength and self-worth.

EMPOWERMENT PROFILE

These, then, are the eight empowerment behaviors. Where does your organization fit in this profile? What do you do to empower others? Table 7.2 presents an Empowerment Profile for you to complete about your organization. As you look at this profile, know that few of us are fully to the left. Sadly, most of us reside well to the right. The effective manager, however, will accept this challenge of the fourth building block of richer organizational climates and create events and occasions

Table 7.2   Empowerment Profile (Organizational Version)

People have important work to do.											People have trivial, uninteresting work to do
People have complete discretion to do their work.	|	|	|	|	|	|	|	|	|	|	People have no discretion to do their work
People have all resources needed to do their work.	|	|	|	|	|	|	|	|	|	|	People have no resources to do their work.
People receive much recognition and praise.	|	|	|	|	|	|	|	|	|	|	People receive no recognition or praise
People feel their survival is completely in their own hands.	|	|	|	|	|	|	|	|	|	|	People feel their survival is in the hands of others.
People have all the needed task skills.	|	|	|	|	|	|	|	|	|	|	People have no task skills
People receive much recognition and praise.	|	|	|	|	|	|	|	|	|	|	People work separately and apart from others.
The organization welcomes surprise	|	|	|	|	|	|	|	|	|	|	The organization hates surprise.

acceptable

that will move her organization from the right side to the left of the empowerment profile.

CASE EXAMPLE OF PACIFIC CITY

Let us briefly describe one city's experience to illustrate the principles we have discussed. The Empowerment Profile for Pacific City government (table 7.3) shows an organization wherein people have important work to do and have the skills to do that work. That is the positive side

Table 7.3   Empowerment Profile (Organizational Version) (Pacific City

Left	1	2	3	4	5	6	7	8	9	10	11	Right
People have important work to do.	X											People have trivial, uninteresting work to do.
People have complete discretion to do their work.				X								People have no discretion to do their work.
People have all resources needed to do their work.								X				People have no resources to do their work.
People receive much recognition and praise.		⋅							X			People receive no recognition or praise.
People feel their survival is completely in their own hands.							⋅	X				People feel their survival is in the hands of others.
People have all the needed task skills.		X										People have no task skills.
People receive much recognition and praise.						X						People work separately and apart from others.
The organization welcomes surprise.										X		The organization hates surprise.

acceptable

of the profile. On the negative side is the reality that people in Pacific City are isolated from one another and receive very little praise. The organization prefers things to be predictable, but often they are not. The employees have little expectation that survival is in their own hands and limited resources or discretion to do their jobs. Pacific City has serious needs for more empowerment.

Prescriptions for Empowering Practices and Activities

But what should Pacific City do about its profile? The remainder of this chapter offers practical suggestions, actual scenarios, and words of wisdom to guide the venture of empowering people in an organization. Pacific City or any other organization can promote empowerment by means of activities and events like those described.

Principle 1. You Empower People When You Give Them Important Work to Do.

While Pacific City fared well on this item, some work still remains to be done. Most organizations pose greater challenges. Here are some practices and activities to help you on the way.

The Business Card   In Japan, a primary symbol of recognition and the importance of work is the business card. "Visiting cards [business cards] play an important part in Japanese life and are exchanged on every conceivable occasion" (Baedeker's). Moreover, an established etiquette governs the transfer of cards to a colleague, client, or potential supervisor. The manner in which these cards are traded and accepted denotes the power given to people.

Who would imagine the power symbolized by a card so small? Just ask anybody who does not possess one! While Americans do not exchange cards as often or with as much ritual as the Japanese, the power of that card is well accepted. To have a business card means you are involved in important work, work that others need to know about. It means you are important enough that others must have a way to contact you.

The power of the business card crystallized for me in my capacity as principal of a new elementary school. I decided to have business cards printed for each staff member. The cards were presented to the staff at a holiday celebration. One staff member was heard saying "Now I know I belong to this team!" Another said, "I have never felt as much like a professional as I do today." And yet one more, with tears in her eyes shared, "This is the best present I could have received. I can hardly wait to hand them out over the holidays to show everyone the importance of my job."

The staff continued to talk about their first business cards long after receiving them. They had been included in what had seemed, to those who felt they did not belong, to be a very exclusive club. They had felt like outsiders looking in on people engaged in important work.

A caution: A business card alone will not suffice to empower the people on your team. It has the desired effect only if the work assigned is truly important to the effectiveness of the organization.

Employees who perceive their job as important are more likely to go the extra mile. Managers who acknowledge the importance of the work in which their employees engage also forge strong links to organizational goals. Following are additional ways of expressing this importance to members of your team.

MBWA: "Management By Walking Around" Let your staff know why each job is important. Seems simple enough. Just write down (1) the names of all your employees, (2) when you last spoke individually with each one, and (3) and the content of that interaction. We asked the Pacific City managers to assess how many contacts were made to reinforce the importance of an individual's work to the organization.

Delegating for Growth When an important task faces you, to whom do you delegate the assignment? Does the same employee always take responsibility? Delegate important work to someone new, and you will find that you have empowered one more person, strengthened your team, and advanced the goals of the organization. One more person becomes willing to "go the extra mile." Use this simple chart to assess task assignment on your team.

After each task, designate who would be assigned to complete it. Now ask yourself the following questions.

- Is everyone in your organization represented?
- Is the same person called on to complete many projects?
- Who is not represented? Why?
- Who could be asked to do more?
- Are assignments equitable?

Principle 2. You Empower People When You Grant Them Discretion in Doing Their Work.

Pacific City is below the acceptable line for this principle. To determine whether this situation is due to skill level of the employee or to distrust of management, some empowering activities might include the following.

Delegating for Growth

Name	Task	Importance of Task 1 (high) to 10 (low)

Task Sociogram   Brainstorm a list of tasks or assignments that come up in your organization. A sample is provided.

Report to the mayor pro tem ⎯⎯⎯⎯⎯⎯⎯⎯⎯⎯⎯⎯⎯

Prepare presentation to the city council ⎯⎯⎯⎯⎯⎯⎯⎯⎯

Write grants ⎯⎯⎯⎯⎯⎯⎯⎯⎯⎯⎯⎯⎯⎯⎯⎯⎯⎯

Visit mobile home parks ⎯⎯⎯⎯⎯⎯⎯⎯⎯⎯⎯⎯⎯⎯

Matching Skill Needs to Professional Development   Analyze the skills of each employee on the following chart.

Name	Strengths	Weaknesses	Needs

Now develop a professional growth plan based upon the analysis. Ask yourself the following questions.

- Do several employees need the same skill development?
- Do I encourage employees to grow professionally?

- Are required resources available?
- Do I ask them what *they* think they need?

Checking and Changing Management Style   Analyze your own management style with each employee.

Name	Checking	Confirming	Trusting	Reason
M. Jones		X		Lateness
P. Dole			X	Good work
L. Verne	X			Incomplete

Now identify a small project that could be given to an employee who has been constantly checked on. Practice being a confirming manager for this project. With an employee you usually confirm, practice being a trusting manager.

Discretionary Resources Checklist   Similar to the second activity just preceding is the Discretionary Resources Checklist, on which employees show the discretion they believe they need to do their optimum job and the discretion they perceive to be granted.

Resource	Discretion Needed	Discretion Granted
Money		
Time		
Personnel		
Facilities		
Energy		

Principle 3. You Empower People When You Give Them the Resources to Do Their Work.

As noted earlier, money is not the only resource. Often the other resources—time, energy, facilities and people—empower people. Pacific City is troubled with inadequate resources. In such a situation, ensuring adequate resources becomes a primary function of all managers. The following suggestions can be implemented in any organization, public or private, to empower employees.

Sharing the Vision   Articulate and broadcast a clear vision for the organization.

Unearthing Employee Needs   Schedule time at every staff meeting to assess each employee's need, whether that be an extension of time, additional funds, or assistance from other people. When this process is included as a regular feature of staff meetings, it is nonthreatening and, in fact, advantageous to every employee.

Problem-Solving Together   Use other staff members to problem-solve a situation. Designate "team time" at staff meetings to solve real or artificial problems. This process will have the added dimension of building a team as each individual learns to assist others.

Taking the Offensive   An empowering manager always looks for ways to garner resources *before* they are needed for specific tasks.

A Buddy System   Does everyone in your organization have someone to turn to when he encounters a problem with a task? Most employees develop an informal help system, but managers can formalize the process so it is open to all. In this way you provide extra energy and more people for every organizational task.

A Mentor System   Identify people with a variety of specialized skills or knowledge to whom any employee may turn as needed. Mentors might rotate or change in number, depending on the scope of the tasks assigned, thus allowing different employees to be empowered at different times.

Work Away from Work   Be flexible about geography. Often a task can be accomplished twice as fast at a different location. For example, must an employee always be at work? Allowing employees to choose the location for a task empowers them to use time efficiently and effectively.

A case in point is the classroom teacher. Often teachers are given assignments outside of their classroom responsibilities. Among these are writing grants, designing curriculum, selecting textbooks, and writing report cards. These tasks *could* be completed on site, but only with many interruptions as phone calls come in, substitutes need help, or a student has an important question. I have found that sending these teachers off campus to work brings them back energized and confident in the outcome of the assigned task. They increase their productivity without an increase in resources. This scenario also becomes viable in business. Recently we worked with a group of managers from a communications company. Even though we were in a separate building on site, they continued to run back to their offices at every break—just to check on things. Had they been off site, this would not have been possible. Their energy would have focused on the task at hand rather than on the multiple responsibilities that awaited them.

In *The Third Wave* (1980), Toffler forecast a new phenomenon—the "electronic cottage." More and more people, he predicted, would work from their homes. While very few people will perform most of their work in this fashion, many employees could complete some of their work in various locations—at home, off site, on the road. Freedom of geography can expand resources of time and energy.

Principle 4. You Empower People When You Give Them Praise and Recognition.

Of all the principles discussed, this one probably receives the most "of course" comments. Everyone knows the necessity of praise and recognition; how to give them sometimes baffles us. Expanding the fifth resource—energy—is all but impossible without this principle. Yet praise and recognition are almost nonexistent in Pacific City.

The following suggestions are merely jumping-off points. No doubt you will add to this list and become a source of ideas for your colleagues.

Patting your Employees on the Back

- Do it verbally.
- Do it in writing. Examples: Thank-you notes; special memo pads for writing quick positive messages; cards designed especially for this purpose
- Do it visually. Examples: Stickers; tokens of accomplishment; flowers

In one organization, every management meeting began with awards of red apples to select managers who had successfully accomplished an activity or task. The apples were always the shiniest and largest red apples available. The gesture, fairly inexpensive, was a highly effective display of recognition by the superintendent in front of peers.

- Do it consistently, but not predictably.
- Regularly provide moments of recognition, but avoid reducing them to predictable "Employee of the Month" Awards.
- Remember that unexpected flowers mean more than expected ones.

A Formal Awards Program

- Several computer programs on the market make many kinds of certificates. Hand these out to deserving employees. You will find them posted on office walls and shared with colleagues over and over again.
- "Picture This" is a program that can be started within any organization. Keep an instant camera around and take pictures of outstanding employees. Post them in prominent places.
- Present your employees with gifts that reinforce their place in the company: a desk clock with the company logo, a coffee mug, a visor, or a T-shirt. Whatever the item, the recipient is made to feel special—to know that someone "up there" recognizes what he or she does and how important he or she is to the organization.
- Extend an employee's lunch hour for a few minutes. Employees are so accustomed to eating on the run and in short segments of time (usually thirty minutes) that prolonging a lunch just by fifteen minutes is appreciated as recognition of good work. Employees in both public and private organizations accept the award of time as one of the highest forms of recognition.
- Ask an employee's opinion. While you are walking around your organization, get into the habit of asking questions. People love to talk. If they feel like an expert, or if the topic is a hobby or their family, they will talk forever. As you walk away, chances are the employee feels inflated and energized by your sincerity and interest.
- Use an organizational newspaper to publicize the successes of

employees. A regular column might feature noteworthy staff members.

Principle 5. You Empower People When You Make Them Feel That Their Survival Is in Their Own Hands.

Once again Pacific City comes up short. The employees feel dependent, rather than empowered. How can the City Manager successfully implement the principle of survival?

Taking Notice   Highlight successful activities that move the organization toward its goals. A CEO I worked with took every opportunity to announce employees' accomplishments and to describe how those accomplishments would guarantee the continuing success of the organization. At board meetings, he highlighted employees whose actions were making the organization great. He consistently reinforced his conviction that the high reputation of the organization endured because its employees were committed to excellence. He knew almost every employee by name and made sure that during his frequent visits, he spoke to each of a recent accomplishment. This organization is cohesive, and the employees put in many extra hours toward self-improvement. By going beyond praise to relate their contributions to organizational prosperity, the CEO has empowered those employees with a sense that their survival lies within their own hands.

The Trusting Environment   Build a trusting environment. Survival does not mean sink or swim alone. Employees in some organizations know that if they do not meet some—often secret—standard of success, they will be gone on Friday! By contrast, a manager who empowers also builds trust with and among employees. Impart a work environment that makes it clear that the effort put forth by each employee is a necessary ingredient in the successful operation of the organization.

Listening First   Refrain from jumping in quickly to solve problems. Managers need to stop and listen. Oftentimes an employee knows precisely how to solve a particular problem and just wants the idea validated. Managers who are quick to respond with a solution prevent workers from solving—eventually even from considering how to solve—problems.

Problem-Solving Sessions   Bringing a variety of employees together to solve problems cooperatively not only supports Principle 3, as noted above, but also reinforces Principle 5. A real problem might be production-oriented. Perhaps the organization has experienced a drop in the number of widgets produced. Teams are asked to develop new ways to boost production. In the process, employees learn that they are a part of solutions and hence are responsible for their own survival.

Identifying Needed Resources   Encourage employees to determine their own resource needs. How will they make the task happen? What do they need?

An Accountability Atmosphere   Emphasize that accountability is the inevitable partner of responsibility. Employees must be willing to accept error and failure and move forward to more effective behaviors.

Suggestion Box   Establish a suggestion box or suggestion board. This is an old idea that still works! Encourage employees to articulate how they think their tasks or end products could be improved. Then investigate and respond with appropriate retooling. Be sure to give the credit to the employee!

"Employee Suggestions Take on Weight in Lean Times," blared a headline in the *Los Angeles Times* on September 15, 1991. The article chronicled savings of $2.3 billion in organizations "implementing 328,000 employee ideas." The article went on to say that employees typically offered suggestions to obtain recognition, not cash. According to one prolific suggester, "You have to get people on the bandwagon. When you start making suggestions, you start thinking about your job differently."

Principle 6. You Empower People When You Enhance and Build Task Skills.

Pacific City is above the acceptable range on this principle. Nevertheless, a variety of activities could further empower their workers. For example, as already noted under Principle 2, ongoing educational opportunities for work groups at all levels can be matched to skill needs of each employee. Other ways to build task skills include the following.

Modeling   Model the skills to be acquired by employees. In the presentation of Principle 6 earlier in this chapter, you read how demonstrating lessons in the classroom both announced and demonstrated the skills a principal expected of her teachers.

Mentors   Mentors were mentioned earlier as a way to expand your available resources. This occurs as new or retrained employees turn to mentors for assistance. Mentors provide a risk-free situation in which an employee may try out a new skill and have it critiqued without fear of evaluation. The mentor is especially valuable where adults are anxious about computers and other technologies. It is vital that employees have a support system as a new skill is learned.

Job-Alike Groups   Promote job-alike groups at established times during work hours. Employees facing similar tasks can offer suggestions and share new learnings with co-workers as new skills are introduced and applied. In a school organization, grade-level or content-area teams would meet to share ideas, plan curriculum, and problem-solve. In an office, the clerical staff, sales group, or the like would come together.

Principle 7. You Empower People When You Encourage Them to Work in Teams.

The employees of Pacific City spend most of their working time in isolation, an arrangement that saps energy and discourages active problem-solving. Many of the suggestions offered previously in this chapter promote the teamwork principle. Recall the following:

- Work away from work (Principle 3)
- A buddy system (Principle 3)
- A mentor system (Principles 3 and 6)
- Problem-solving sessions (Principles 3 and 5)
- Job-alike groups (Principle 6)

Other ideas are as follows . . .

Interdependent Teams   Oftentimes it is valuable to form interdependent work teams to foster creativity. For example, a team member from advertising will propose different ideas than will workers entrenched in production.

Team Process Skills

- Develop norms for operating (see chapter 3).
- Rotate leadership role in regular or committee meetings.
- Ask yourself: Does the team work together? If not, why not?

A Conducive Environment   Restructure the environment to stimulate and support teamwork. Changes may vary from rearranging the furniture to revising the list of departments or persons called together. To increase the number of minds addressing problems and issues, you might assign two employees part-time to a task that might otherwise have been handled by one employee full-time.

Principle 8. You Empower People When You Welcome Surprise.

The managers of Pacific City hate surprises. As a result, they have stifled their employees. Organizations can encourage surprises, thereby empowering and energizing people, in both simple and complex ways.

Encouraging Risk   For surprises to pop up, people must be encouraged to take risks. If you take only the Cook's tour, few if any surprises will occur along the way. Fashion a Build a Better Mousetrap Day in your organization. Encourage employees to try out new ideas, whether they consist of actual inventions or nontraditional ways of doing things. Include everyone in this celebration—most important, yourself.

Risk Buttons   Provide "risk buttons" that read "Congratulations for taking a risk!" Or create some other surprising acknowledgment of the idea-generators in your organization.

Employee Newsletter   Publish an employee newsletter that chronicles the ideas of the moment. Remember to report end results; for example, "Dollars Saved; Bonuses Announced" or "Idea Fails, but Generates New Approach."

Reflection and Rumination   Do not expect employees to come to you with pat answers—and by the same token, do not give them pat answers. Let them see you ruminating over possibilities!

Recognition   Give recognition not just for its own sake (Principle 4) but to signal the behaviors you are looking for. "This surprise has been brought to me by (name), who was not afraid to try!"

CONCLUDING NOTE

Empowerment begins from a philosophical commitment to building the power of individual employees. In too many organizations, however, that is where it also ends. To empower, managers must perform behaviors that concretely expand the capabilities and energies of employees. To empower, you must turn belief into action.

CHAPTER 8

Inspiring Intrapreneurship

Ben Franklin, Thomas Edison, Tom Watson, Susan B. Anthony, Martin Luther King Jr., and Doug DeVore—what comes to mind when you think of these people? That they are well-known men and women of dynamic ideas and undying commitment to change? Well, maybe Doug DeVore is not well known, but all the others manifested a documented dedication to innovation.

Most organizations need more people with a hunger for ideas. Typically, however, they wait for the Ben Franklins and the Thomas Edisons to come along, but this is a once-in-a-lifetime event. Perhaps organizations would do better if they set up environments in which the Doug DeVores of the world might invent and flourish. Inducing a wealth of creativity in the average person may serve us far better than waiting for the Watsons or Anthonys to come along. Inspiring intrapreneurship addresses precisely that issue—fostering creativity. Up to this point, we have discussed a variety of enriching activities that make organizations more effective, satisfying, and rewarding. Intrapreneurship has a slightly different intent—to spark innovation and new directions in organizational goals and outcomes. It focuses on enriching the cognitive side of organizations.

RESOURCES

Money, facilities, people, time, and energy have always been important resources to advance organizations and teams. We have become accustomed to managing these five resources; however, there is a sixth resource. As we have moved from the industrial into the information age, this new resource—*ideas*—has emerged. Ideas have become products in themselves or, at least, the means to new products. Consequently, universities are dedicated to creating new ideas. Hospitals and health services grow only as they find new cures and new technologies—or new ways to apply old cures and technologies. Governmental agencies no longer have the luxury of raising new revenues; instead, they seek new ideas to manage dwindling resources while meeting demands for increased services. In an information age, the business of business *is* to create new ideas and new technologies. In fact, across all organizations, as other traditional resources become more scarce and competition more intense, ideas are critical to survival. The dilemma is: How do you spark new ideas? . . . How do you induce creativity? While these questions yield no simple answers, the literature on creativity does intimate that we cannot make people creative; rather, we allow them to be creative. That is to say, human beings are already creative; all you need do is establish environments that let creativity emerge.

This reality has come home to me many times over the years, but the first time it hit me was probably the most memorable. In 1970, when I was an administrator at a university, I took an extended summer workshop called "Administration and the Arts." I had written a "fair deal" of poetry at the time and felt quite accomplished. The workshop experience was frustrating because most of the participants had little sense of the arts, little insight into the meaning of creativity. They had been assigned to take this workshop. To my mind, they were "typical" managers. One of the requirements of the workshop was that we come back together a month later to share some creative piece each of us had crafted in the interim. I wrote some poetry but dreaded sharing it with a group of people who had little sensitivity to the arts. I remember walking downstairs into the studio/classroom to see the participants' "creative" attempts . . . and . . . they were wonderful! Many of my workshop colleagues had risked new genres or new approaches. I had had no idea they could be so creative. I felt two inches tall. They were all Gullivers, and I was a Lilliputian. While I had fumed about their lack of creativity, while I was mentally chiding them for their shallow understanding, while I expected less than nothing—the workshop leader had not. He set up an environment where they could try, where creativity could emerge.

I realized then, as I have since been frequently reminded, that to assume people lack creativity or that someone must "make" them creative is to adopt an arrogance that is founded in untruth and wholly unproductive. Conversely, if you assume that people are creative and that your job is to establish conditions that nurture new ideas and approaches, then you are genuinely effective. Your reward will be a flood of new ideas and approaches. We all have our own workshop stories. Sometimes they involve our colleagues, sometimes our spouses, often our children. How many times have you been amazed by the creativity of children? How often do we give them freedom to demonstrate it?

INTRAPRENEURSHIP DEFINED

It is toward this purpose—inducing new ideas—that this chapter is pointed. It is toward creation of intrapreneurs that this building block is constructed. Let us begin by defining "intrapreneur":

The intrapreneur is the person within an organization who is the counterpart of the entrepreneur. This person actively and recurrently seeks out new ways and approaches to solve current problems, avert impending threats, or seize upon emerging possibilities. This person is a lightning rod for change and innovation, a fountain of creative ideas.

The term "intrapreneurship" emerged as a new concept in the early 1980s (Pinchot 1985), having been coined in parallel to the term "entrepreneurship." In the decade of the 80s there crystallized an imperative for innovation in both new and existing organizations. Earlier, in a stable, closed-system world, innovation had been unnecessary. But in a turbulent world, as described in chapter 1, innovation became the lifeblood of survival. Existing, established organizations were desperate to spark internal innovation. Several structural mechanisms were attempted, among them quality circles, innovation societies, and "skunk works." All were attempts to induce creativity in employees. All share three assumptions:

1. Organizations need innovation to survive.
2. People's creativity is not made by others; it is released.
3. What leaders do in an organization is a greater predictor of creativity than what other people do. Leaders establish settings; settings release creativity.

Validation

This intrapreneurship construct was validated by the work of Odell (1995) and Rutherford (1994). Odell writes, "This study has over-whelmingly established that intrapreneurship leads to dramatize change." Intrapreneurship is a method to build a strong innovative team.

LEADERSHIP FOR INTRAPRENEURSHIP

With these assumptions in mind we suggest that managerial leadership is the keystone to the sixth resource—ideas. Further, we suggest that leadership to induce intrapreneurship falls into three phases:

- Setting the scene
- Priming ideas
- Moving to decision/implementation

Setting the Scene

In previous chapters, we enumerated the steps or elements inherent in a particular management practice. So, too, in this case we list nine elements to help you set the scene for intrapreneurship (table 8.1).

Be Flexible Enough to Waive Standard Policies

Taylor, in her study of intrapreneurship (1980), found that the single most predictive characteristic of innovative organizations was the lead-

Table 8.1.   Setting the Scene

1. Be flexible enough to waive standard policies
2. Avoid home-run mentality
3. Provide discretionary resources
4. Create cross-functional teams
5. Hold intra celebrations
6. Encourage voluntary intrapreneurship (Do not appoint intrapreneurs)
7. Recognize time-intensive realities
8. Bombard strengths
9. Avoid territoriality

ership's willingness to waive standard policies in the face of innovation. The opposite, however, is too often true. Faced with a new idea, we frequently say, "That is against policy" or "I don't think our policies will allow us to do it."

For managers within long-established settings, waiving policies may be the most difficult element—not because it is prohibited but rather because of the traditional and consistent systems that characterize these institutions. As a manager, I often sat with groups preparing to write "innovative" grant proposals. It often took hours of brainstorming and discussion before ideas emerged that were different enough to require a waiver of standard policy. We are often blocked by our own history.

Another issue that suggests caution is concern about organizational safety. In this litigious society, we have become better and better at "managing risk"—a phrase that has become a euphemism for avoiding lawsuits. To this end, we avoid the unusual and the unprecedented. While this mindset may reduce lawsuits, it also inhibits innovation. To spark new ideas and innovations, leaders must be flexible. They must recognize that some things cannot fit neatly between the lines and—most important—that the future of the organization may well be concealed in the something that does not fit.

Of course one must manage risk—but in both directions. In other words, for the sake of innovation you should reduce risk in some ways and increase it in others. For example, best- and worst-case analyses help reduce risk; waiving standard policies may increase it.

Avoid Home-Run Mentality

I am reminded of a mother at my son's Little League games. This overbearing mother always yelled, "Hit a homer, Corey!" Her yells echoed throughout the park and on every field. She was the penultimate embodiment of the overbearing Little League mother. "Hit a homer, Corey!" And, of course, Corey never did hit a homer. Expect too much, and you get very little.

On the other hand, creativity will emerge when you keep your expectations within reasonable bounds and when you focus on clearly defined, relatively small innovations. Major innovations may emerge, too, but not because you were expecting them. You hit a homer not by trying for it but when you simply try to meet the ball and drive a solid single. A researcher finds a cure for cancer not by seeking the remedy directly but by taking arduous, incremental steps toward understanding what advances and what restrains the disease. These smaller ideas churn until the solution materializes. To unleash creativity, encourage small, focused, innovative efforts.

Provide Discretionary Resources

As discussed in chapter 7, you empower people when you give them discretion over resources. To be more specific, when you give employees control over funds, facilities, people, and time, you also induce them to try new ideas, new combinations, new approaches. Conversely, you reduce creativity when people feel they have no control over resources. They may have great ideas, but if they have no way to try them out, to bring them to reality, they become discouraged and disillusioned. If they can do nothing with their ideas, why even bring them up? Note the corollary to this premise: A way to "hide" in a bureaucratic organization is to lack control over resources. People cannot be held accountable for resources over which they have no control. A person hiding is a person who contributes little. If you do not want people hiding in your organization—more, if you want new ideas and possibilities—give people resources so they can run with their ideas. The resources need not be lavish—the necessary and appropriate level of resources varies from organization to organization and situation to situation. In general, however, moderate resources will spark possibilities, open the possibility of success, and excite intrapreneurship.

Create Cross-Functional Teams

New companies are, by their nature, small and integrated. Everybody does everything. In a brand new business, you do not have the luxury of saying, "That's not my department." You do whatever it takes to survive. When I began my adult work life, I worked in a small tire store. I was the "sales manager." I soon discovered that that meant changing snow tires in the winter rush season, writing credit reports, acting as the service manager, and even occasionally managing sales.

As organizations enlarge and become better established, they set up differentiated departments and functions to promote expertise through specialization.

However, as Lawrence and Lorsch (1969) point out, institutions need *both* differentiation *and* integration. The latter often becomes lost. Department heads talk to one another but not to department members. In a city, for example, the planning director talks to the parks and recreation director, but seldom do project planners talk to the park workers. The result—planned developments in which parks do not serve people's needs. Without organizational integration, creativity is stifled. Therefore, one keystone to intrapreneurship is the small, cross-functional team—that is, the group with representation from multiple departments. By gathering people from different divisions, you garner a totality of perspectives and a chance to test ideas across the full organization. Clusters of unlike minds create novel ideas.

Hold Intra Celebrations

Most of the existing literature focuses on formal rewards. However, as Kinlaw (1991) writes, "The informal process of appreciation and celebrating can be a very powerful tool for developing superior work teams." Further stressing the value of informal celebrations, Kinlaw continues, "Informal awards are likely to have more impact on people than formal ones." Coming together to celebrate success heightens excitement and induces intrapreneurship. Three caveats are in order, however:

1. Do not rely on formal awards such as employee-of-the-month programs. They are too narrow and tend to invite invidious comparisons. As we noted earlier, spread celebration widely.
2. Do not overlook the dull parts of the organization. In a university, no one ever discusses the registrar's office unless there is a problem. The registrar's office is virtually invisible in the organization. When things go well, that fact is ignored; when they go badly, everyone notices. In your organization, the analogous department may be data processing or quality control. Remember

that all parts of the organization are important and deserve celebrations.

3. Do not be afraid of too much celebration, as long as that celebration focuses on products and ideas related to the success of the organization. "We know that too little appreciation impacts negatively on performance. We have not the slightest hint that too much appreciation has a negative impact on performance" (Kinlaw 1991, 110).

Climates that include excitement and celebration foster intrapreneurship. Remember: Joy*ful* cultures are more powerful than joy*less* ones.

Encourage Voluntary Intrapreneurship

Never appoint intrapreneurs; always allow them to volunteer. Creativity does not bubble up on cue or by edict. It springs from people ready for ideas and blossoms at different times for different people. Like most of the wonderful things in life—love, love-making, friendship, "ah-ha" experiences, the perfect job, peak insights—creativity comes when you are ready inside, not when it fits neatly into a schedule. Moreover, people who choose a project are committed to it. Choice deepens the reservoir of the fifth resource—energy. Example: Have you ever tried to get your children to do something you knew was good for them? More likely than not, they were lackadaisical and mediocre in their performance. But when they found their niche, even you, their parent, were amazed by their energy and devotion. Choice is a powerful and wondrous component of creativity. Support people who want to be intrapreneurs. Compel no one; encourage everyone.

Recognize Time-Intensive Realities

Change takes time. The creativity that sparks change also takes time. Most major universities expect their faculty, particularly junior faculty, to publish. Yet they also load these new instructors with troops of counselees and a plague of committee assignments. The result is not insufficient time to write but lack of time to deliberate and ponder and create. Creativity is decidedly inefficient. Time to contemplate is important for intrapreneurship.

Some of my most creative academic years have occurred when I had few classes and was between consulting engagements. During those quieter periods, I had time to sit back and ask "What if . . . ?" The same is true in any organization. How inappropriate, then, for a CEO, seeing a manager with his chair tipped back and feet on the desk, to assume that that manager is not working. People may do their most creative work while walking around airports or sitting in a park or leaning back with their feet on the desk. And while I might write an article in a day, or a book in a month, that article or book is the product of months and years of experience, mulling, reflection and "ah-ha" flashes of insight. Intrapreneurship takes time.

Bombard Strengths

As Blanchard and Johnson (1982) have advised, catch people doing something right. Creative organizations bombard people with a sense of success; they focus on the strengths of individuals. To operate from strength is to operate in freedom. Freedom releases creativity. We described a strength-bombardment exercise in chapters 2 and 5. Whenever we use this activity, we are amazed at how touched people are by it. Most workers have few opportunities to hear about their strengths. Even if they know or suspect their own strong points, hearing them mirrored in the words of others makes them far more real, powerful, and enriching.

At one staff meeting I had each person place a 3x5 card on a neighbor's back so that everyone had one on. I gave them five minutes to walk around and write something positive on five or six of their colleagues' cards. I could not get them to stop! When at last they were seated, one teacher exclaimed, "Forget the meeting. . . . I'm ready to invent the future. . . . My colleagues think I'm great!" A wild consensus followed.

If you do not believe us, try an experiment. For one month, bombard one employee with appreciation, with descriptions of the strengths she brings to the organization. Make sure she feels good about her strengths. Pick a second employee (not a close co-worker of the first) and treat this person neutrally (a few compliments, a few negatives). At the end of the month, sit down and discuss new ideas and approaches with each. Which one do you suppose will be more creative and open? Knowledge of personal strength sparks a sense of freedom which, in turn, releases creativity.

Avoid Territoriality

"Mind your own business!" "That's not your area!" "Trespassers will be prosecuted!" "Beware of the dog!" "Keep off the grass!" These are but a few of the uninviting signs in life. They tell us to stick to our own territory, to stay on our own turf. As noted above, however, the more we stay to ourselves, the less insightful we can be. This truism applies to cultural and interpersonal as well as organizational understandings. The greater the integration of different parts, the greater the insight and the greater the array of ideas.

An additional point of import goes beyond insight, however. Problems are, by their nature, seldom intradepartmental or unidimensional. They span departments, disciplines, and functions. New approaches, then, must inevitably cut a swath across many departments and functions. Consider Sherlock Holmes, who was undaunted by the "keep out" signs of the world. He followed clues to their logical ends and solutions, wherever they took him. Likewise, intrapreneurs need sufficient freedom within their organizations to pursue ideas across multiple turfs. Seldom can you stay on your own turf and solve a problem. "The game is afoot," and intrapreneurs must have the freedom to finish it.

Summary and Application

In attending to these nine elements, you set the scene for intrapreneurship—that is, you establish an environment wherein people will venture forth freely to seek new ideas and new approaches. By setting such a scene, you achieve leadership for innovation and creativity. The obverse is equally true. If you fail to set this scene, you cut off creativity and new ideas.

This building block, inspiring intrapreneurship, differs from the preceding four in that it occurs on multiple, sequential levels. In other words, you cannot move to level two until you have reasonably satisfied level one (see figure 8.1). If you are either medium (a score of 22 to 43) or high (a score of 44 to 55) in setting the scene, as measured by the Intrapreneurship Quotient Instrument (see table 8.2), you are ready for priming ideas.

Let us look at a real organization we diagnosed. We will call it Elite University (see table 8.3). Elite U scored 30 on the Intrapreneurship Quotient Instrument. This was sufficient to move on to the next level. However, their results indicated weaknesses in two areas: resource allocation and willingness to waive standard policies. Their strengths lay in openness to ideas, cross-functional teams, and realism. Theirs was not a strong level 1 intrapreneurship, yet it was high enough to warrant examining level 2, priming ideas.

Priming Ideas

The second phase of intrapreneurship calls for priming ideas. This phase involves management activities that foster new ideas. In phase one, you prepared the soil. In phase two, you water and fertilize the ideas to allow them to sprout. This phase includes seven elements (see table 8.4).

Encourage Brainstorming

An adage in the business world advises "ask for the sale." Similarly, if you want ideas, you must ask for them. A number of structured activities accomplish this purpose. These include brainstorming, charades, nominal group technique (see Harvey, Bearley, and Corkrum 1997),

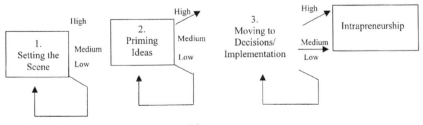

Figure 8.1 Moving to Intrapreneurship

Table 8.2.   Intrapreneurship Quotient Instrument, Part I: Setting the Scene

To what degree does your organization:

	Not at all				To a very great extent
Show willingness to waive standard practices to encourage innovation	0 1 2	3	4	5	
Allow potential intrapreneurs to operate by a different set of rules	0 1 2	3	4	5	
Encourage small/focused innovative efforts	0 1 2	3	4	5	
Provide discretionary funds for intrapreneurs to use	0 1 2	3	4	5	
Provide other budget resources for intrapreneurs such as released time, personnel, etc.	0 1 2	3	4	5	
Create cross-functional teams	0 1 2	3	4	5	
Hold celebrations for intrapreneurs and potential intrapreneurs	0 1 2	3	4	5	
Encourage intrapreneurs to volunteer ideas and time	0 1 2	3	4	5	
Recognize the time demands of intrapreneurship	0 1 2	3	4	5	
Compliment employees on their strengths and successes	0 1 2	3	4	5	
Allow intrapreneurs to operate outside their own turf	0 1 2	3	4	5	
Total:					

and carouseling. Many of them are included in the University Associates (Pfeiffer Group) material described earlier or in such books as Schmuck and Runkel (1985). Whatever technique you use, remember these six points:

1. Record the ideas publicly. Make sure everything is written on a flip chart or board or on some other obvious public display. In that way people can see that their ideas have been recorded.
2. Transcribe and distribute the ideas to all. Do not just record the ideas publicly, but type them out and distribute them to everyone in the group or organization so participants' have a permanent

Table 8.3.   Intrapreneurship Quotient Instrument, Part I: Setting the Scene (Elite University)

To what degree does your organization:

	Not at all				To a very great extent	
Show willingness to waive standard practices to encourage innovation	0	1	**2**	3	4	5
Allow potential intrapreneurs to operate by a different set of rules	0	1	**2**	3	4	5
Encourage small/focused innovative efforts	0	1	2	3	**4**	5
Provide discretionary funds for intrapreneurs to use	**0**	1	2	3	4	5
Provide other budget resources for intrapreneurs such as released time, personnel, etc.	0	**1**	2	3	4	5
Create cross-functional teams	0	1	2	3	**4**	5
Hold celebrations for intrapreneurs and potential intrapreneurs	0	1	**2**	3	4	5
Encourage intrapreneurs to volunteer ideas and time	0	1	2	3	**4**	5
Recognize the time demands of intrapreneurship	0	1	2	3	**4**	5
Compliment employees on their strengths and successes	0	1	2	**3**	4	5
Allow intrapreneurs to operate outside their own turf	0	1	2	3	**4**	5

Total: 30

Selected values in bold

record for themselves. If the ideas are few, distribute them to the whole organization. If the ideas are many, complex, or unclear, distribute them only to team members.

3. Do what you say you are going to do. Whatever you commit to do with the ideas, follow through. You discourage people if you tell them you will do something but do not do it.

4. Review ideas. Before the next session, review the ideas previously generated. You need not be limited by them, but you should monitor them.

5. Whatever priming strategies you use, use them repeatedly. Foster-

Table 8.4.   Priming Ideas

1. Encourage brainstorming	4. Examine surprises/look for lacunae
2. Promote Management by Walking Around (MBWA)	5. Think simple and focused
	6. Stay close to clients
3. Network/visit	7. Provide common information

ing creativity is not a one-shot deal. The more often you brainstorm, the more interesting the ideas.

6. Allow some time to pass between sessions. People need time to reflect, mull over, and/or act upon previous ideas.

If you want ideas, you must ask for them. When you ask for them, do so in a systematic, but interesting manner.

MBWA

A great myth that clouds our understanding of innovation is that great ideas emerge only from the minds of highly creative and intelligent people. In reality, however, great ideas spring from the minds of great listeners. Drucker's book *Innovation and Intrapreneurship* acknowledges this reality. But more vivid for me was a testimonial dinner we attended for a client of ours who was a wonderfully inventive guy. I do not remember his exact words, but they ran something like this:

> I appreciate all the good things you've said about me tonight. But I'm afraid I'm a bit of a fraud. That packaging idea wasn't all mine; all you folks in marketing and operations led me to that. And that new product line was really Ted Smith's doing. [He continued with other examples.] I never really have been very creative. I'm just a good listener who had great employees. God gave me two ears and one mouth. He taught me how to use my ears before he taught me how to talk.

This man was a great listener—and a great leader. He was one of the leaders Peters and Waterman talked about; he believed in Management By Walking Around (MBWA). But remember there is more to MBWA than "walking around." Its importance lies not in your glorious presence amid the troops, but in your asking questions and then listening to the answers. If you want to prime creative ideas, ask questions. Ask them of people where they work, not where you work. Go to their offices, go out to the assembly line, go into classrooms, ask questions—and then listen to the answers. You need not convert them to your perspective, nor do they need to convert you to theirs. Simply listen and store away.

Network/Visit

Another way to prime ideas is to encourage people to visit other sites and operations and to network with associates in the field. Looking at your operation through the lens of other people and their modes of operation both affirms many of your current procedures and also sparks new ideas.

Remember, however, that the new ideas discovered through these associations should be mulled over and redefined by your own people. Too many managers see something they like elsewhere and simply adopt it, only to find that it does not fit smoothly in the new context. To avoid this mistake—always adapt, never adopt. This maxim yields greater ownership along with better understanding. Another caveat for those attending association meetings or conferencing with colleagues is that their intent should be to generate ideas, not just to "schmooze." Unless this purpose is clear, building relationships supplants idea creation at many a conference or association meeting. Network and visit to gather ideas.

Too often, though, we fail to give people the time necessary to formulate ideas that percolate from networking or visiting. As a result, an idea or innovation is lost as the crush of daily work sets in. Plan that time! Allow employees a day after a visit or conference to ruminate, to mentally try out new creations, or to bounce ideas off colleagues. Time for creative thinking leads to successful innovation.

Examine Surprises

Organizations face an interesting paradox. They have been created in society to bring order and routinization to social functions. Organizations exist to bring control and order out of potential chaos. As consumers we know what to expect of our organizations and then expect to receive it. When I go to McDonald's, I expect a relatively mediocre hamburger in jig time. The slower the service, the unhappier I become. At Scandia, on the other hand, I expect excellent food and leisurely service. If they try to rush me, I become angry. I know what to expect from each. So pervasive is this notion that Holiday Inn built an entire advertising campaign on "no surprises." All in all, most organizations are systematized around consistency, avoiding surprise.

The paradox arises from our turbulent world, a world in which roles and functions change. Surprises occur. Organizations that attempt to guard against such surprises are, at minimum, courting reverses or, in the worst case, doomed to failure. Effective, innovative organizations look for surprises. They examine the lacunae, the gaps between what they expected and what they got. These gaps offer opportunities for innovation (Drucker 1985).

Given this reality, we propose that you regularly ask, as part of your weekly or monthly meetings, "What surprises have we had this week/month?" Those surprises may be positive or negative; they may pose potential threats or possible opportunities. Either way, it is important to examine your organization for surprises and to ask how and why they occurred. In examining surprises, you escalate the likelihood of new ideas.

Think Simple and Focused

As noted earlier, you want to avoid a home-run mentality; you should expect little ideas rather than major solutions. It follows that you must encourage your people to "think simple and focused." It is a paradox that as you aggregate a series of small, focused ideas, you may arrive at larger, more fundamental answers.

As a graduate of Princeton University, I have always been fascinated with the work of Robert Oppenheimer. In reading about the evolution of the atom bomb and the history of atomic energy in general, I am continually impressed by the myriad of small discoveries that eventually added together to create one of the most awesome and fearsome "discoveries" of mankind. Atomic power was not a single, giant brainstorm, but a million small ones. Ben Franklin never set out to discover electricity; he merely pursued a series of "what ifs." If you want the big idea, encourage your organization to "think simple," "think focused"—and then keep on thinking.

Stay Close to Clients

Other ideas come from the clientele of systems and services. For businesses, they are customers; for universities, they are students; for hospitals, they are patients; for government, they are citizens. Whatever the term, they are the same people. They do (or, in some cases, do not) receive an expected service or product, and they can tell you much about it. They live in the same turbulent world as organizations; consequently, they face emerging needs that neither you nor they ever expected. When you stay close to your customers, you learn their needs.

The opposite is equally true. I remember a million-dollar grant that I was asked to evaluate by the National Endowment for the Humanities. This Midwestern university had surveyed students, looked at other schools, and consulted with experts. So in 1969 it received a million-dollar grant to establish a center for social activism. Through various problems and shortfalls, the project was delayed, so the center did not open until 1973. By that time, the Midwest was no longer a bed of social activism. The center was no longer needed. But the university went ahead as originally planned. As might be expected, the center was an abject failure. The only surprise was that the university was surprised. In the four years since the original grant, the faculty had never collected another student survey, never looked at other schools. The university lost sight of its clients. In turbulent times, awareness of changing client needs is an ongoing process. One-shot assessments seldom work. Ideas do, indeed, germinate as we talk with our clients—but we must talk with them frequently.

Provide Common Information

A final source of good ideas is a well-rooted knowledge of your own operations. This statement may seem strange, yet our experience indicates that many members do not understand just how their own organizations work. As they learn more about the organization, they have more ideas to suggest for its operation. Even more consequential is the dark side of this principle. The more you hide or fail to share information about the organization, the more suspicious people become. They assume a hidden conspiracy, and their suspicions increase toxicity in the organization. Share information widely and you will not only dispel suspicion, you will also invoke increased understanding and new ideas.

The importance of this guideline came home to me dramatically when I was assigned as principal of a school under construction. I began writing a Tuesday letter home to the community to keep them updated on the status of construction. In the letter I also rambled on about happenings in the portable school, information about the staff, and progress of various parent/staff committees. Two years later, I was still writing! Staff and community came to expect this missive. When a week was skipped, I heard about it! Information is power. Information builds trust. Information encourages innovation.

Summary and Application

By regularly priming ideas, you gain innovative notions and creative approaches to problems. But to get ideas, you must ask for them, and ask for them regularly. As a measure of your efforts to prime ideas, the second level of intrapreneurship, you might complete the second section of the Intrapreneurship Quotient Instrument (table 8.5). A score of 14 or above on this section of the IQI suggests that you have adequately responded to priming ideas.

Surprisingly, this is where Elite University fell down (table 8.6). You would think a university, by its very nature, would take action to spark ideas, but Elite did not. Management—assuming that "ideas would just come from the faculty; after all, they *are* the faculty"—took no responsibility for fostering new possibilities. This was a major weakness, and we advised them to become more proactive, particularly in asking questions (MBWA), networking, sharing information, and looking for surprises. When they had succeeded in doing a bit more of these activities, they were ready for level 3—doing something with the ideas they had.

Table 8.5.   Intrapreneurship Quotient Instrument, Part II: Priming Ideas

To what degree does your organization:

	Not at all				To a very great extent	
Encourage employees and teams to brainstorm on a recurrent basis	0	1	2	3	4	5
Encourage managers to walk around your organization and ask questions of employees	0	1	2	3	4	5
Provide an opportunity for employees to visit other sites, go to conferences, or participate in other networking	0	1	2	3	4	5
Look for gaps between what is expected and what actually happens, then examine reasons why these gaps occur	0	1	2	3	4	5
Encourage thinking about small, simple focused issues	0	1	2	3	4	5
Urge employees to be close to the clients/customers and listen to their ideas/needs	0	1	2	3	4	5
Provide access to information from all departments and levels	0	1	2	3	4	5
Total:						

Moving to Decisions/Implementation

The third level of intrapreneurship calls for decision-making and the implementation of ideas. The eight elements of this final stage in inspiring intrapreneurship are displayed in table 8.7.

A common complaint when we begin a strategic planning process is, "Why should we do all this work? No one ever did anything with the last plan." The failure to actively move forward and implement ideas is fatal to intrapreneurship. Creating ideas is fun; implementing them is not. But both are important.

Implementation requires careful planning. While ideas can be created through "bull sessions," brainstorming, and other relatively informal strategies, successful implementation needs a formal process. "Who will be involved in the implementation?" "How will we implement?" and "What resources do we have and need?" are oft-heard questions. For ideas to find their way into the organization, we suggest

Table 8.6.   Intrapreneurship Quotient Instrument, Part II: Priming Ideas (Elite University)

To what degree does your organization:

	Not at all				To a very great extent
Encourage employees and teams to brainstorm on a recurrent basis	0	**1**	2	3	4	5
Encourage managers to walk around your organization and ask questions of employees	0	**1**	2	3	4	5
Provide an opportunity for employees to visit other sites, go to conferences, or participate in other networking	0	1	2	**3**	4	5
Look for gaps between what is expected and what actually happens, then examine reasons why these gaps occur	0	**1**	2	3	4	5
Encourage thinking about small, simple focused issues	0	1	**2**	3	4	5
Urge employees to be close to the clients/customers and listen to their ideas/needs	0	1	**2**	3	4	5
Provide access to information from all departments and levels	0	**1**	2	3	4	5

Total: 11

Selected values in bold

that effective managers use the following eight elements as they move toward implementation.

Encourage Bounded Risk

Change and new ideas do entail risks, but those risks must be bounded by probability. The chance must be greater that this *will* work

Table 8.7.   Moving to Decisions/Implementation

1. Encourage bounded risk	5. Recognize intrapreneurs
2. Make incremental decisions	6. Allow time for success
3. Avoid handoffs	7. Multiply ownership
4. Reward success/accept failures	8. Monitor progress,

than that it *will not*. Great, long-term innovators understand this and calculate carefully that the odds are in their favor. Both Drucker (1985) and Harvey (1990) describe the importance of bounded risk—that is, limiting risk to acceptable boundaries. When risk associated with a new idea is perceived as large, when new ideas are seen as threatening individual or organizational survival, creativity among members of the organization will inevitably be curtailed. Who wants to cause their own demise or that of the organization that employs them? Las Vegas is a good example of bounded risks. Most people go to Las Vegas intending to risk X dollars—and they stick to their resolve. They risk their money, but only to a certain degree. Luckily for gambling-house owners, a few are die-hard risk-takers with no boundaries who eventually lose it all. They are not risk-takers; they are fools.

Make Incremental Decisions

In change theory, we talk of the theory of small wins (Harvey 1990). This theory advises that change occur in baby steps because otherwise, people cannot succeed. Thus, if you structure a change as a series of smaller changes, you significantly increase your chances of success. This principle applies to teaching and learning any new skill. In mathematics, one builds from counting to addition and subtraction to algebra. You learn to drive a car by learning to steer, then shift, then use the gas judiciously, and so on. Parents learn to raise children through a never-ending series of small, often painful lessons. Whenever we fail to master the small lessons, the larger lessons are far more difficult.

Therefore, to implement any new idea or innovation, you need to create a series of smaller decisions and implementation steps. Do not try to do too much too fast. Make incremental decisions and succeed.

Avoid Handoffs

"What a great idea, Nancy. That's exactly what we need to do. Tim, why don't you take Nancy's idea and run with it?" If you were Nancy, how would you feel? Probably deflated and undermined! In implementing intrapreneurial ideas, it is important to allow the originator of the idea to carry it out. Too often, however, we take one person's brainchild and hand it off to someone else. Perhaps this error arises from a misinterpretation of differentiation—a false belief that some people are idea people while others are implementers. When you differentiate assignments on this basis, you also lose people's commitment to the idea and hunger for its success. People who come up with an idea should be allowed to carry it to full realization.

We remember a fast-food outlet that was brainstorming ways to change its image. One of the employees, Sarah, who was developmentally delayed (Down's Syndrome), suggested wearing signs to tell people "how much we care about them." The other employees jumped on the idea and ran with it, but none of them included Sarah. So she quietly went off on·her own. She looked hurt and dejected, but she was no quitter. While the others spent an hour working on logos and slogans, she was in the other room drawing and cutting. The others finally settled on printing up aprons with the motto "Service with a Smile." Later that afternoon, when they all got together to work the evening shift, Sarah showed up with a big, round cardboard button pinned on her apron that said, "I love to cook for you." She was a hit with the customers and the author of a new slogan. When we fail to involve the authors of ideas with their implementation, we lose human energy—we waste the fifth resource. Sarah was developmentally delayed, but she had much to offer. Too often we fail to trust others to lead from idea to implementation. Avoid handoffs. Expand energy.

Reward Success/Accept Failures

This element, rewarding success and accepting failures, has two dimensions. The first is to tie clear rewards to each incremental step of success. Unless both chang*ers* and chang*ees* anticipate payoff, they will not sacrifice the time and struggle to implement an innovation. In motivation and change theory, this concept is called "valence"— people do things for which they expect payoff. Consider: One definition of insanity is "being self-abusive." Therefore, if we ask you to implement a new idea that is going to demand more work or skills or energy or time without offering any hope of payoff, you would be clinically insane to say "yes." Sane people look for payoffs—not necessarily in money, but perhaps in recognition, achievement, or interpersonal relations. Whatever the payoff, however, it must have worth for the changee. If you do not reward successful implementation of new ideas, the old ideas will stay in place.

The second dimension of this element is accepting the reality that mistakes and errors will occur. Nothing new ever works as we expect it to. A new computer system, a new curriculum, a new building, a new product line, a new reporting system—all are subject to errors and mistakes. As discussed in chapter 2, toxic organizations are those that do not tolerate error. When you attempt to be error-free and risk-free, you will also be creativity-free.

Recognize Intrapreneurs

We need not give much space to the importance of this element. We have recounted its significance throughout this book. Let it suffice to emphasize five points:

1. Tie recognition to worker behavior. Make clear what ideas and innovative approaches are being celebrated; too often recognition is given to people as individuals, not to their achievements.
2. Encourage workers to recognize one another. Mutual peer appreciation is more powerful and long-lasting than appreciation from superiors. Certainly both are desirable, but peer celebration especially enhances positive organizational climate.
3. Avoid the plague of superiority. Sometimes recognition is viewed as a designation of superiority. When this happens, the target of recognition often becomes equally a target of enmity.
4. Recognition can be public or private, so do both. Send individual, private messages and give public recognition.
5. Remember that the point of recognition is facilitating implementation of creative ideas, not self-aggrandizement or currying favor.

Allow Time for Success

Effective intrapreneurial climates allow people time to get the job done. Elective boards are notable for their failure to recognize this reality. While campaigning for votes, politicians are wont to promise quick, instant answers to complex questions. They promise what the system cannot deliver. School board members are particularly subject to this impatience. They expect to see instant reversal of test scores or other quick victories. The reality of innovation is that it takes time, not just to create but also to implement. Therefore, intrapreneurs must establish realistic action plans that entail:

- Clear, incremental steps for idea implementation
- A clear time line for achieving each step
- The person to carry out each step
- The resources needed for each step

When action plans are clear and realistic, innovation can happen. Chandler (1990) found that action plans were the most consistently overlooked component in change efforts. When action plans are absent, implementation is inevitably limited.

Multiply Ownership

Earlier in this section on implementation we urged organizational leaders to avoid handing off ideas, taking them away from their originators and turning them over to others. The mirror principle is also important. If an innovation enjoys commitment and involvement from no one other than the intrapreneur, you sow seeds of major problems that will bloom at a later date. What happens, for instance, if that intrapreneur leaves or loses institutional support? The idea or innovation also loses its place in the organization. You cannot have a long-term successful organization where new approaches or ideas are solely dependent on particular individuals. It is critical to long-term change to expand proprietary ownership of the change (Harvey 1990). The best medium for this is an implementation team. While the intrapreneur might have originated the idea, she should have a team around her to implement it. This practice not only distributes the work load, it also expands investment and ownership. If the idea is a product of an intrapreneurial team rather than one person, we recommend that, in order to enlarge ownership and extend insights, you expand that team slightly to form an implementation group.

Monitor Progress

Nothing ever comes off as planned. Given this reality, it is important for organizational leaders to monitor progress of innovative efforts. Without such a radar system, the organization cannot adjust as it must. If you do not monitor progress, you cannot make the alterations to ensure that the new idea becomes integrated into the organizational system. It is not enough to watch just the initiation of an idea or approach; one must follow through until full institutionalization has taken place.

Summary and Application

The elements required to move into decision-making and implementation involve both anticipating, and thus preventing, loss of focus and energy and ensuring maintenance, or institutionalization, of the new idea. Habit is a powerful force that is antithetical to the implementation and institutionalization of new ideas ranging from answering machines (I still know people who refuse to speak to a machine) to governments (witness the months of seething turmoil in formerly communist regimes). But if you set the scene, prime ideas, and then move to decisions and implementation as we have described, you will both generate and realize the fruits of creativity. The third section of the Intrapreneurship Quotient Instrument (see table 8.9) allows an organization to diagnosis its success in the third and final stage of that process.

In examining the Elite University case once again (table 8.10), we found an organization that was doing a reasonable job of moving to decision and implementation. The university's greatest strengths were avoiding handoffs, giving recognition, and providing adequate time. Its greatest weakness, however, lay in monitoring progress. As they had in the stage of priming ideas, management assumed that everything would "go as planned." They did not recognize the need for a radar system. All in all, Elite was a reasonably intrapreneurial university that assumed a little too often that innovation would "happen naturally." They were advised to become more assertive in following through to establish and maintain an intrapreneurial climate to induce ideas and innovation.

As you apply the Intrapreneurship Quotient Instrument to your own organization, the following summary of score interpretation may prove useful (table 8.8). The summary for Elite University appears in table 8.11.

CASE EXAMPLES OF INTRAPRENEURSHIP QUOTIENT INSTRUMENT

On the following pages we have provided two additional case examples of the Intrapreneurship Quotient Instrument. This instrument is designed to assess the twenty-seven elements associated with organizational intrapreneurship. In addition, each phase shows a Level Index Score. Before reading the analysis we have provided for each organization, return to the chapter and decide for yourself the diagnosis and prescription necessary to increase their intrapreneurship levels.

Now you are ready to assess your own organization. Which phase are you in? Have you moved too quickly to the next phase? We strongly suggest that you give the IQI to others in your organization. Are there discrepancies among the respondents or with your perceptions—or are you synchronized?

Staid City

On pages 223–25 (tables 8.12–8.15) is the Intrapreneurship Quotient Instrument for Staid City. Remember to develop your own diagnosis and prescription as you review the instrument.

Staid City: Diagnosis and Prescription

Staid City was a truly toxic organization. It had been fraught with political strife, and employees were often caught in the cross-fire. The

---

Table 8.8. Intrapreneurship Quotient Score Interpretation

	Low	Medium	High
Setting the scene	0–21	22–43	44–55
Priming ideas	0–13	14–27	28–35
Decisions/implementation	0–17	18–35	36–45

Table 8.9.   Intrapreneurship Quotient Instrument, Part III: Moving to Decisions/Implementation

To what degree does your organization:

	Not at all				To a very great extent	
Encourage intrapreneurs to take limited, reasonable risks	0	1	2	3	4	5
Make incremental decisions and plans	0	1	2	3	4	5
Allow intrapreneurs to carry out their own ideas	0	1	2	3	4	5
Reward success	0	1	2	3	4	5
Realize that mistakes are an inevitable part of innovation	0	1	2	3	4	5
Give recognition to intrapreneurs	0	1	2	3	4	5
Provide reasonable time for a new project to show success	0	1	2	3	4	5
Expand the ownership for innovations to a larger group	0	1	2	3	4	5
Monitor/evaluate the progress of the innovative effort	0	1	2	3	4	5
Total:						

city faced significant fiscal problems and high rate of staff turnover. The way out of this morass of problems, the city manager suggested, was new ideas and innovative approaches. The entire city council agreed with this premise, yet the organization did little to make that premise a reality. They did little to set the scene for innovation. Indeed, they were weak on almost every element of that first phase of inspiring intrapreneurship. This failure in setting the scene had a significant impact on priming ideas, which had an even lower score. The one area of success, albeit limited, was their commitment to listening to citizens' needs. This strength, however, was often short-circuited by political machinations. No matter where you looked in this organization, you could find little to encourage enthusiasm or joy or excitement over new possibilities. Staid City government lacked positive energy.

To reverse that trend, we advised the following:

Table 8.10.   Intrapreneurship Quotient Instrument, Part III: Moving to Decisions/ Implementation (Elite University)

To what degree does your organization:

	Not at all				To a very great extent	
Encourage intrapreneurs to take limited, reasonable risks	0	1	2	**3**	4	5
Make incremental decisions and plans	0	1	2	**3**	4	5
Allow intrapreneurs to carry out their own ideas	0	1	2	3	**4**	5
Reward success	0	1	2	**3**	4	5
Realize that mistakes are an inevitable part of innovation	0	1	2	**3**	4	5
Give recognition to intrapreneurs	0	1	2	3	**4**	5
Provide reasonable time for a new project to show success	0	1	2	3	**4**	5
Expand the ownership for innovations to a larger group	0	1	**2**	3	4	5
Monitor/evaluate the progress of the innovative effort	0	**1**	2	3	4	5

Total: 27

Selected values in bold

- At the very minimum, Staid City can spark creativity and encourage intrapreneurial behavior within the organization by providing a new focus on recognition of employees.
- Second, Staid City must deal with the need to provide employees with more discretionary funds. This can be accomplished through financial, time, or personnel considerations.
- Next, the introduction of cross-department teams or meetings will

Table 8.11.   Intrapreneurship Quotient Instrument, Part IV: Summary (Elite University)

	Score	Low	Medium	High
Setting the scene	30	0–21	22–43	44–55
Priming ideas	12	0–13	14–27	28–35
Decisions/implementation	27	0–17	18–35	36–45

Table 8.12.   Intrapraneurship Quotient Instrument, Part I: Setting the Scene (Staid City)

To what degree does your organization:

	Not at all					To a very great extent
Show willingness to waive standard practices to encourage innovation	0	1	**2**	3	4	5
Allow potential intrapreneurs to operate by a different set of rules	0	1	**2**	3	4	5
Encourage small/focused innovative efforts	0	1	**2**	3	4	5
Provide discretionary funds for intrapreneurs to use	**0**	1	2	3	4	5
Provide other budget resources for intrapreneurs such as released time, personnel, etc.	0	**1**	2	3	4	5
Create cross-functional teams	0	**1**	2	3	4	5
Hold celebrations for intrapreneurs and potential intrapreneurs	0	**1**	2	3	4	5
Encourage intrapreneurs to volunteer ideas and time	0	1	**2**	3	4	5
Recognize the time demands of intrapreneurship	0	**1**	2	3	4	5
Compliment employees on their strengths and successes	0	**1**	2	3	4	5
Allow intrapreneurs to operate outside their own turf	0	**1**	2	3	4	5

Total: 14

Selected values in bold

induce creative thinking and an understanding of how the whole operation works, thus allowing opportunity to work outside of an individual's "own turf."

By addressing just these three areas, Staid City will be able to move forward on the other items in setting the scene, then proceed successfully to priming ideas. When they administer the IQI again, even though they will still be focused on setting the scene, they can expect to find higher scores in both that area and the subsequent phase, priming ideas.

Table 8.13.   Intrapraneurship Quotient Instrument, Part II: Priming Ideas (Staid City)

To what degree does your organization:

	Not at all				To a very great extent	
Encourage employees and teams to brainstorm on a recurrent basis	0	**1**	2	3	4	5
Encourage managers to walk around your organization and ask questions of employees	0	**1**	2	3	4	5
Provide an opportunity for employees to visit other sites, go to conferences, or participate in other networking ⋅	**0**	1	2	3	4	5
Look for gaps between what is expected and what actually happens, then examine reasons why these gaps occur	0	1	**2**	3	4	5
Encourage thinking about small, simple, focused issues	0	1	**2**	3	4	5
Urge employees to be close to the clients/customers and listen to their ideas/needs	0	1	2	**3**	4	5
Provide access to information from all departments and levels	0	**1**	2	3	4	5

Total: 10

Selected values in bold

California Technical Systems Corporation (CTSC)

CTSC: Diagnosis and Prescription

California Technical Systems Corporation (CTSC) was an exciting, yeasty environment to work in. It was high in all the phases of intrapreneurship with particularly strong attention to leadership of change, rewards and celebrations, and attention to customers. Perhaps its biggest negative was its impatience. The CEO wanted change immediately, expecting everyone to absorb new ideas and approaches into existing workloads.

This was a problem for many CTSC employees. They loved the organization but their pace of innovation was slower than that of their CEO.

Table 8.14. Intrapraneurship Quotient Instrument, Part III: Moving to Decisions/Implementations (Staid City)

To what degree does your organization:

	Not at all					To a very great extent
Encourage intrapreneurs to take limited, reasonable risks	0	1	**2**	3	4	5
Make incremental decisions and plans	0	1	2	**3**	4	5
Allow intrapreneurs to carry out their own ideas	0	1	2	**3**	4	5
Reward success	0	**1**	2	3	4	5
Realize that mistakes are an inevitable part of innovation	**0**	1	2	3	4	5
Give recognition to intrapreneurs	0	**1**	2	3	4	5
Provide reasonable time for a new project to show success	0	1	**2**	3	4	5
Expand the ownership for innovations to a larger group	0	**1**	2	3	4	5
Monitor/evaluate the progress of the innovative effort	0	**1**	2	3	4	5

Total: 14

Selected values in bold

We encouraged the CEO to take on the motto "Things Take Time" to allow the employees to absorb the innovations that were coming at breakneck speed. By providing the time necessary to institutionalize these changes, the CEO found that employees took greater risks and continued the intrapreneurship environment that had become the CTSC culture (see tables 8.16–8.19 for the Intrapreneurship Quotient Instrument for CTSC).

Table 8.15. Intrapraneurship Quotient Instrument, Part IV: Summary (Staid City)

	Score	Low	Medium	High
Setting the scene	14	0–21	22–43	44–55
Priming ideas	10	0–13	14–27	28–35
Decisions/implementation	14	0–17	18–35	36–45

Table 8.16.   Intrapreneurship Quotient Instrument, Part I: Setting the Scene (CTSC)

To what degree does your organization:

	Not at all				To a very great extent
Show willingness to waive standard practices to encourage innovation	0	1	2	3	**4**	5
Allow potential intrapreneurs to operate by a different set of rules	0	1	2	**3**	4	5
Encourage small/focused innovative efforts	0	1	2	3	**4**	5
Provide discretionary funds for intrapreneurs to use	0	1	2	3	**4**	5
Provide other budget resources for intrapreneurs such as released time, personnel, etc.	0	1	2	3	**4**	5
Create cross-functional teams	0	1	2	3	4	**5**
Hold celebrations for intrapreneurs and potential intrapreneurs	0	1	2	3	4	**5**
Encourage intrapreneurs to volunteer ideas and time	0	1	2	3	4	**5**
Recognize the time demands of intrapreneurship	0	1	**2**	3	4	5
Compliment employees on their strengths and successes	0	1	2	3	**4**	5
Allow intrapreneurs to operate outside their own turf	0	1	2	3	**4**	5

Total: 44

Selected values in bold

CONCLUDING NOTE

Ideas are made possible only with energy and enthusiasm throughout the organization. If you want ideas and innovation, you must create and manage an intrapreneurial environment. Such an environment releases individual energy and creativity.

Table 8.17.   Intrapreneurship Quotient Instrument, Part II: Priming Ideas (CTSC)

To what degree does your organization:

	Not at all				To a very great extent	
Encourage employees and teams to brainstorm on a recurrent basis	0	1	2	3	**4**	5
Encourage managers to walk around your organization and ask questions of employees	0	1	2	3	4	**5**
Provide an opportunity for employees to visit other sites, go to conferences, or participate in other networking	0	1	2	3	**4**	5
Look for gaps between what is expected and what actually happens, then examine reasons why these gaps occur	0	1	2	**3**	4	5
Encourage thinking about small, simple, focused issues	0	1	**2**	3	4	5
Urge employees to be close to the clients/ customers and listen to their ideas/needs	0	1	2	3	4	**5**
Provide access to information from all departments and levels	0	1	2	3	**4**	5
Total: 27						

Selected values in bold

Table 8.18.   Intrapreneurship Quotient Instrument, Part III: Moving to Decisions/Implementations (CTSC)

To what degree does your organization:

	Not at all					To a very great extent
Encourage intrapreneurs to take limited, reasonable risks	0	1	**2**	3	4	5
Make incremental decisions and plans	0	1	2	3	**4**	5
Allow intrapreneurs to carry out their own ideas	0	1	2	3	**4**	5
Reward success	0	1	2	3	4	**5**
Realize that mistakes are an inevitable part of innovation	0	1	2	3	**4**	5
Give recognition to intrapreneurs	0	1	2	3	**4**	5
Provide reasonable time for a new project to show success	0	1	**2**	3	4	5
Expand the ownership for innovations to a larger group	0	1	2	3	**4**	5
Monitor/evaluate the progress of the innovative effort	0	1	2	3	**4**	5
Total: 33						

Selected values in bold

Table 8.19.   Intrapreneurship Quotient Instrument, Part IV: Summary (CTSC)

	Score	*Low*	*Medium*	*High*
Setting the scene	44	0–21	22–43	44–55
Priming ideas	27	0–13	14–27	28–35
Decisions/implementation	33	0–17	18–35	36–45

CHAPTER 9

Connecting the Blocks

We began this journey into people-building with a tale of a Thracian king who ordered his ministers to build a magnificent palace for him. Let us now take liberties and suggest a different version of that tale.

An ancient tale tells of a Thracian king who governed his realm with love for his people and a passion to enrich their lives. He asked little for himself, only the chance to use his power for the benefit of the realm. The people, in turn, loved their king, and in joy and celebration they decided to build him a magnificent palace as a monument to his beneficence. For five years they toiled, and when they were done, it was as magnificent as any king could want. It was made of the sturdiest marble and the strongest Greek stonework. On the third day that the king lived in the palace, there was a sudden storm. The winds blew and rain pelted the palace. Amid the thunder and lightning the edifice stood firm, although much around it collapsed in ruin. After the storm the king invited those who were homeless to stay in the palace until they rebuilt. This palace continued to survive many other storms and travail.

Then one day, in great old age, the king died. There was another storm that night, and this time the palace began to shake and crack. The minister and governors were shocked and bewildered. They asked, "Why now? Surely the king's death could not have caused this." But the people knew. "This edifice was built on love and it was the king's belief in the people that held it together." The queen then stepped forward to take her rightful place as Thracian leader. She quickly surveyed her realm and, discovering cracks and crevices, began the task of restoring and revitalizing the palace and its people. She worked among them, offering reassurances and energy as the palace surpassed its previous magnificence and became the envy of every ruler in the surrounding areas. When the rulers convened for the formal coronation ball, they turned to the queen and asked, "How were you able to inspire such a faithful following that would toil and sacrifice to rebuild this palace?" The wise queen responded, "It is not the palace that was restored. The power of brick and mortar pales in the face of the power of belief and commitment. When you build your palaces on people, on families, on city states, they will last."

As you have surely guessed, the moral is that when you build your organizations with an eye to the five building blocks we have described, they will last. The power of an empowered people who build positive environments and norms, who effectively manage conflict and induce creative tension, who work collaboratively in teams, and who explore new opportunities and creative alternatives is far greater than any organizational chart or systems approach to management. The people infrastructure is the most powerful of all the infrastructures we have.

A second moral is that each new leader must build or rebuild the palace, regardless of how benevolent, supportive, and nurturing the previous leader was. Effective organizations are not self-sustaining, nor is their energy. Just as the queen had to move in quickly to survey the changes brought on by the storm, so must every organizational leader. Whether you are new to an organization or continuing your tenure, you must take time periodically to survey your realm. Organizations in today's world exist in an open system and are living and growing entities for that reason. With each new leader, with every change, comes the necessity to cycle through the building blocks, assuring that the mortar is in place and the cracks refilled.

CONCEPTUAL FRAMEWORK

In our fable, the demise of the king did not cause the demise of the Thracian people. A modern-day leader would assess the organization just as the queen had, using the five building blocks of a strong organizational climate:

- Team-building
- Norm-setting
- Conflict management

- Empowerment
- Intrapreneurship

The diagram in figure 9.1 depicts the interrelationship of these factors. At the core is team-building. It is the most all-encompassing of the five. The others branch out from it. In one direction are empowerment and intrapreneurship. They are the most proactive, seizing upon opportunities and building new capacities and potentialities. In the other direction are norm-setting and conflict management, which operate more in the domain of organizational maintenance. They deal with the threats and problems that plague an organization. All five blocks include proactive and reactive elements, all of which require attention. The wise manager addresses both recurring organization maintenance functions and the need to expand, invent, and explore new dimensions. These five disparate building blocks, which were presented as separate components for diagnosis and development, are in reality linked and interdependent. To address only one leaves your organization weakened and imbalanced. In concert, however, they offer balance, managerial power, and a highly effective organizational climate. If, on the one hand, your organizational health is tied most closely with new visions and fresh possibilities, you will do more with empowerment and entrepreneurship. If, on the other hand, your need is to deal with an environ-

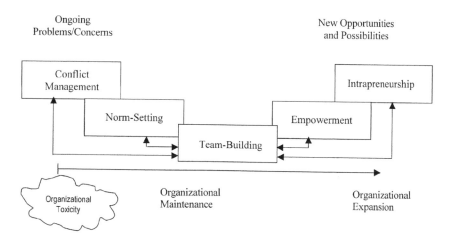

Figure 9.1   Building Blocks of Rich Organizational Climate

ment that is already toxic, you will rely more on norm-setting and conflict management. Team-building is a strong building block for both scenarios.

The building blocks are meant to be used in a way that is different for and appropriate to each organization; hence, assessment tools have been provided. Initially, some organizational leaders find it helpful to move serially from one to another. As your organization moves toward expansion, you may loop or cycle through selected building blocks.

Energy Climate Checklist

To meld these five building blocks, we suggest a climate checklist for managers. You have already worked with separate instruments for assessing each area, but this checklist combines all five building blocks. Table 9.1 shows the elements of the checklist. As you consider the health of your organization, read through the checklist and mentally note those factors that are weak or absent. Post this checklist on your bulletin board or over your desk. Refer to it periodically as a reminder of the elements that build teams by building people.

ENERGY CAUTIONS

As we have repeatedly stated in this book, the fifth resource—energy—may be the most important of all. It expands and enhances all the others. There are some cautions about energy, however, that the astute leader must keep in mind:

Energy Is Not Self-Renewing

Once you achieve a situation where people feel energized, do not believe that it will maintain itself without careful management. You must work at the renewal of energy.

Energy Is a By-Product

You cannot get people to love you by saying, "Love me"—or to trust you by saying "Trust me." Love and trust are by-products of other

Table 9.1.   Energy Climate Checklist

Have you given or created:

_____ A sense that work is important
_____ Common identity/focused vision
_____ Common tasks
_____ A sense of success
_____ Willingness to be accountable
_____ Discretion to perform tasks
_____ Adequate resources
_____ Necessary skills to perform tasks
_____ Realistic expectations
_____ Flexibility and responsiveness
_____ Tolerance of errors/risk
_____ Opportunity to network
_____ Cross-functional teams
_____ Encouragement of voluntary intrapreneurship
_____ Appreciation of surprise and creativity
_____ Clear definition of members' roles
_____ Balanced roles
_____ A common base of information
_____ Opportunities for brainstorming/creative solutions
_____ Mutual trust
_____ Acceptance of conflict
_____ Understanding of kinds of conflict and effective resolution strategies
_____ A willingness to confront conflict openly
_____ A healthy questioning/listening environment
_____ A healthy level of stress
_____ Clear, visible norms
_____ Processes for norm-setting
_____ An acceptance of group structure
_____ Recognition and praise
_____ A sense of joy and celebration
_____ A sense of accountability

activities or behaviors. The same is true of energy. It is the by-product of joy, self-confidence, success, hope, perspective, curiosity, and passion. You cannot tell a group to become energized; they must first experience other insights and emotions, then draw energy from within themselves.

Energy Requires Direction

Energy without purpose or direction dissipates. To be effective, energy needs leadership that channels and directs it toward organizational purposes. The Keystone Kops and a highly trained SWAT team both have energy, but the former is scattered and ineffective while the latter is poised, focused, and effective.

Energy Can Be Scary

Coming into highly charged dynamic organizations can be very scary. It means people must turn up their energy levels. Many employees fear they cannot meet the demands of such a charged organization. Low-energy settings offer comfort—few demands and little change. What they lack in vibrancy and excitement, they make up in peace and calm. These settings do not survive well in an open-systems world, but they *are* comfortable.

Energy Is Exhausting

No individual or group can operate forever at the peak of energy. We all need points of stability and respite from the challenges of exciting, dynamic organizations. We need periodically to call time out to allow our systems to mend and regenerate for future cycles of enthusiasm and growth.

Energy Is Not Enough

If all you have is energy, then you are doomed to fail. You also need people, facilities, money, time, and ideas. These five resources allow you to focus energy constructively.

Throughout this book we have described ways to create effective teams and build powerful people. We have focused on expanding energy and organizational effectiveness. Such organizational development must keep in mind the realities of energy and growth—the demands placed on you, the leader—because you must

- Work at it
- Create joy, self-confidence, success, hope, perspective, curiosity, and passion
- Provide leadership and direction

- Be prepared for challenges
- Allow time out for personal renewal
- Ensure access to multiple resources

Awareness of these energy cautions allows a leader to channel energy toward significant organizational enhancement.

CONCLUDING NOTE

Although the era of kings and queens has passed, the morals of the fable have not. Your leadership can either destroy what you have built or expand and empower people and teams to reach your vision for the organization. Indeed, the next decades will be a difficult time. The lives and well-being of people everywhere will rest on the effectiveness of all our institutions. We need successful schools, businesses, hospitals, cities, and social service agencies. If you do not succeed as an institutional leader, our institutions cannot succeed. We need you to be effective. We need you to build teams and build people. The choice is yours. Will you be remembered by the people in your organization as the artisan of crumbling edifices or as the builder and renewer of people-empowered, people-empowering structures?

Belief and Vision Statements

Averbeck Company

Preamble

Averbeck Company is more than the sum total of its services and products. It is a company committed to adding greater value to its clients, its investors, and its employees. Averbeck Company is a cost effective and profitable organization known for its integrity and commitment to enriching the lives of the organizations and people it touches. The Tenets that follow represent this commitment:

Tenets

1. We believe that our success comes from each individual in the company being committed to *serving client* needs.
2. We are committed to aggressive growth through innovative and entrepreneurial efforts; growth of the company will come from understanding and meeting *the changing needs* of both current and new clients.
3. We believe that the growth and perpetuation of our company is dependent on the *growth, recognition, and advancement of our employees.*
4. We serve both ourselves and our clients best when we positively work together as a *team.*
5. We believe in *sensitive, honest and timely communication* with our clients, employees, and insurance companies.
6. We are committed to *community service* and support corporate and individual involvement in community activities.

Vision Statement

Averbeck Company will be the leading risk management and employee benefit consulting firm in the Inland Empire and Southern California region. With a $200,000,000 client base, 200 employees, and offices placed strategically throughout the area, the Averbeck Company will provide services and risk management products to medium to large companies throughout the region.

Founded in 1931, Averbeck Company has a long heritage of successful relationships with clients and a commitment to assisting those clients in identifying their needs *and* matching these with a wide array of traditional and non-traditional risk management solutions. Averbeck Company is committed to using a team approach to diagnose and meet client needs.

Averbeck Company works in partnership with its clients by providing consultation and competitively priced insurance products in the following five areas:

1. Commercial Property Casualty,
2. Employee Benefits,
3. Bonds,
4. Personal Lines, and
5. Financial Planning.

Averbeck Company is also committed to public service and believes in contributing to the betterment of people and organizations in its communities.

APPLE VALUES

Empathy for Customers/Users: We offer superior products that fill real needs and provide lasting value. We are genuinely interested in solving customer problems and will not compromise our ethics or integrity in the name of profit.

Achievement/Aggressiveness: We set aggressive goals, and drive ourselves to achieve them. We recognize that this is a unique time, when our products will change the way people work and live. It's an adventure and we're in it together.

Positive Social Contribution: As a corporate citizen, we wish to be an economic, intellectual, and social asset to communities where we operate. But beyond that, we expect to make this world a better place to live. We build products that extend human capability, freeing people from drudgery and helping them achieve more than they could alone.

Individual Performance: We expect individual commitment and performance above the standard for our industry. Only thus will we make the profits that permit us to seek out other corporate objectives.

Team Spirit: Teamwork is essential to Apple's success for the job is too big to be done by any one person. Individuals are encouraged to interact with all levels of management, sharing ideas and suggestions to improve Apple's effectiveness and quality of life. It takes all of us to win. We support each other, and share the victories and rewards together.

Quality/Excellence: We care about what we do. We build into Apple products a level of quality, performance, and value that will earn the respect and loyalty of our customers.

Individual Reward: We recognize each person's contribution that flows from high performance. We recognize also that rewards must be psychological as well as financial, and strive for an atmosphere where each individual can share the adventure and excitement of working at Apple.

Good Management: The attitudes of managers toward their people are of primary importance. Employees should be able to trust the motives and integrity of their supervisors. It is the responsibility of management to create a productive environment where Apple values flourish.

THE FIVE PRINCIPLES OF MARS

1. Quality

The consumer is our boss, quality is our work, and value for money is our goal.

2. Responsibility

As individuals, we demand total responsibility from ourselves; as associates, we support the responsibilities of others.

3. Mutuality

A mutual benefit is a shared benefit; a shared benefit will endure.

4. Efficiency

We use resources to the fullest, waste nothing, and do only what we can do best.

5. Freedom

We need freedom to shape our future; we need profit to remain free.

THE JOHNSON & JOHNSON CREDO

Our Credo

We believe our first responsibility is to the doctors, nurses and patients, to mothers and all others who use our products and services in meeting their needs. Everything we do must be of high quality. We must constantly strive to reduce our costs in order to maintain reasonable prices. Customers' orders must be serviced promptly and accurately. Our suppliers and distributors must have an opportunity to make a fair profit.

We are responsible to our employees, the men and women who work with us throughout the world. Everyone must be considered as an individual. We must respect their dignity and recognize their merit. They must have a sense of security in their jobs. Compensation must be fair and adequate, and working conditions clean, orderly and safe. Employees must feel free to make suggestions and complaints. There must be equal opportunity for employment, development and advancement for those qualified. We must provide competent management, and their actions must be just and ethical.

We are responsible to the communities in which we live and work and to the world community as well. We must be good citizens, support good works and charities and bear our fair share of taxes. We must encourage civic improvements and better health and education. We must maintain in good order the property we are privileged to use, protecting the environment and natural resources.

Our final responsibility is to our stockholders. Business must make a sound profit. We must experiment with new ideas. Research must be carried on, innovative programs developed and mistakes paid for. New equipment must be purchased, new facilities provided and new products launched. Reserves must be created to provide for adverse times. When we operate according to these principles, the stockholders should realize a fair return.

DOCTORAL PROGRAM IN ORGANIZATIONAL LEADERSHIP, DEPARTMENT OF ORGANIZATIONAL LEADERSHIP, UNIVERSITY OF LA VERNE

Tenets

- Collaboration and cooperation are at the heart of leadership.
- The ability to work in teams is critical to successful leadership.
- Leaders must understand and respond to change in order to elevate organizations to meet the needs of the future.
- Theory must be blended with practice. To be relevant and effective, a professional doctoral program must have direct application to the field.
- Passion and commitment are the soul of leadership.
- Statewide networking is important for statewide leadership impact.
- Change and learning occur when work is challenging, interesting and joyful.
- Continuous improvement requires ongoing feedback and self-reflection of one's beliefs, attitudes, skills and behaviors.
- The doctoral program must serve as a partner with the students in their professional life.

- Leaders are entrepreneurial, risk takers and able to build the capacity of self and others.
- Leaders must be able to function effectively in an internal and external political environment.

BRYANT RANCH SCHOOL

A Vision For Bryant Ranch School

Bryant Ranch School will be recognized as an invention center, encouraging students, staff, and community members to continually explore their environment. It will be a problem-solving center that encourages lifelong learning.

Bryant Ranch will offer a unique program for students and be an integral part of the greater community. Its facilities, resources and philosophy will meet the varied learning needs and interests of its diverse participants during the school day and through afterschool activities. Excited, involved learners of all ages will focus on investing in the future.

Bryant Ranch staff will act to heighten students' enthusiasm to become lifelong Explorers. The active involvement of adults as parallel and collaborative learners seeking solutions will be essential in this process.

Bryant Ranch students will be provided programs that will allow them to continually explore the unknown and experience success in their endeavors. Real life issues will become the catalyst for exploring possible solutions and applying a variety of problem solving methods. Students will experience learning through hands on activities, use of technology, and active research in independent and cooperative settings.

These ideas and resources will empower students of Bryant Ranch to focus on knowledge acquisition and creation of new ideas supported by technology. The home and school will work collaboratively to extend the physical base for learning. A nurturing, encouraging, and caring environment will propel our lifelong learners along their educational journey as they "Reflect the Past, Explore the Present, and Invent the Future."

Value Statements

- A positive and caring environment promotes intellectual curiosity, encourages creativity, and provides a balance between team work and independence.
- Promoting high self-esteem is the foundation for all school programs.
- Students and Staff pride themselves in putting forth their best efforts.
- There is a strong sense of community awareness and responsibility.
- Students are provided opportunities to learn about and appreciate the cultural diversity within our community.
- Cooperation among staff, parents, and students encourages open communication and mutual support.
- Learning is celebrated as a lifelong experience.
- Students are recognized for striving towards academic success and appropriate behavior.
- Programs are provided that meet individual student needs.
- Schoolwide programs focus on developing a healthy mind and healthy body.
- Everyone is special.

CATCH THE SPIRIT AT BRYANT RANCH

Bibliography

Barker, Roger. *Ecological Psychology.* Stanford: Stanford University Press, 1968.

Bellack, A. *The Language of the Classroom.* New York: Teachers' College Press, 1966.

Bennis, Warren, and Burt Nanus. *Leaders: The Strategies for Taking Charge.* New York: Harper and Row, 1985.

Blanchard, Kenneth, and Spenser Johnson. *The One-Minute Manager.* New York: Morrow, 1982.

Bryson, John. *Strategic Planning in Public and Non-Profit Organizations.* San Francisco: Jossey-Bass, 1987.

Carpenter, Susan, and W. J. D. Kennedy. *Managing Public Disputes.* San Francisco: Jossey-Bass, 1988.

Cetron, Marvin J. *Schools of the Future: How American Business and Education Can Cooperate to Save Our Schools.* New York: American Association of School Administrators, 1985.

Chandler, Patricia. "The Process of Change in Comprehensive High Schools." Ed.D. diss., University of La Verne, 1990.

Corkrum, Robert L. "Using Team Characteristics to Predict Teamness." Ed.D. diss., University of La Verne, 1996.

Deming, W. Edwards. *Out of the Crisis: Quality, Productivity, and Competitive Position.* Cambridge, MA: Center for Advanced Engineering Study, Massachusetts Institute of Technology, 1986.

Doyle, Michael, and David Straus. *How to Make Meetings Work: The New Interaction Method.* New York: Jove Publishers, 1986.

Drolet, Bonita. "The Power Beneath the Surface: Identifying Behavioral Norms in Schools." Ed.D. diss., University of La Verne, 1992.

Drucker, Peter. *Innovation and Entrepreneurship: Practice and Principles.* New York: Harper and Row, 1985.

Enarson, Harold L. "Art of Planning." *Educational Record* 56 (Summer 1975): 170–74.

Enz, Cathy. *Power and Shared Values in the Corporate Culture.* Ann Arbor, MI: UMI Research Press, 1986.

Filley, A. *Interpersonal Conflict Resolution.* Glenview, IL: Scott Foresman, 1975.

Fisher, Roger, and Ury, William. *Getting to Yes.* New York: Penguin Books, 1991.

Fromm, William. *The Ten Commandments of Business and How to Break Them.* New York: G. P. Putnam, 1991.

Gibb, Jack. "Defensive Communication." *Journal of Communication* XI, no. 3 (1961): 141–48.

Greiner, Larry, and Virginia Schein. *Power and Organization Development.* New York: Addison-Wesley, 1988.

Harvey, Thomas. *Checklist for Change.* Needham, MA: Allyn and Bacon, 1990.

Harvey, Thomas, William Bearley, and Sharon Corkrum. *The Practical Decision Maker.* Lanham, MD: Scarecrow, 2001.

Hersey, Paul, and Kenneth Blanchard. *Management of Organizational Behavior.* Englewood Cliffs, NJ: Prentice Hall, 1988.

Hixson, Susan. "Dealing with Difficult Teachers." Ed.D. diss., University of La Verne, 1997.

Hodgkinson, Harold. *California: The State and Its Educational System.* Washington, DC: Institute for Educational Leadership, 1986.

Isgar, Thomas. *The Ten Minute Team: 10 Steps to Building High Performing Teams.* Boulder: Seluera Press, 1989.

Jamieson, David, and Julie O'Mara. *Managing Workforce 2000.* San Francisco: Jossey-Bass, 1991.

Jones, John, and William Bearley. *Organizational Universe Survey System.* Valley Center, CA: Organizational Universe System, 1991.

Kanter, Rosabeth Moss. *The Change Masters.* New York: Simon and Schuster, 1983.

Kaplan, A. "Power in Perspective." In *Power and Conflict in Organizations,* ed. by R. L. Kahn and E. Boulding. London: Tavistock, 1950.

Kinlaw, Dennis. *Developing Superior Work Teams.* San Diego: University Associates, 1991.

Kipnis, Daniel. "The Powerholder." In *Perspectives on Social Power,* ed. by James Tedeschi. Chicago: Aldine, 1974.

Kouzes, James, and Barry Posner. *The Leadership Challenge.* San Francisco: Jossey-Bass, 1987.

Lawrence, P. R., and J. W. Lorsch. *Organization and Environment: Managing Differentiation and Integration.* Homewood, IL: Richard D. Irwin, 1969.

McClelland, David. "The Two Faces of Power." *Journal of International Affairs* 24, no. 1: 29–47.

Mintzberg, Henry. *Power In and Around Organizations.* Englewood Cliffs, NJ: Prentice Hall, 1983.

Odell, Gayle. "Mastering the Words of Change: Intrapreneurship in California's Distinguished High Schools." Ed.D. diss., University of La Verne, 1995.

Peters, Thomas, and R. H. Waterman. *In Search of Excellence.* New York: Harper and Row, 1982.

Pfeffer, Jeffrey. *Power in Organizations.* Boston: Pitman, 1981.

Pinchot, Gifford, III. *Intrapreneuring; Why You Don't Have to Leave the Organization to Become an Entrepreneur.* New York: Harper and Row, 1985.

Rahim, M. Afzabur. *Managing Conflict in Organizations.* New York: Praeger, 1986.

Roberts, Marc. *Managing Conflict from the Inside Out.* San Diego: Learning Concepts, 1982.

Roberts, Wes. *The Learning Style of Attila the Hun.* New York: Warner Communications Co., 1987.

Rutherford, Garrett. "Dreams That Do: Intrapreneurship in California's Distinguished Elementary Schools." Ed.D. diss., University of La Verne, 1994.

Schmuck, Richard, and Philip Runkel. *The Handbook of Organizational Development in Schools.* 3rd ed. Palo Alto: Mayfield, 1985.

Stauffer, Karen, and Sandra Schultz. "Assisting the Assistant." *Western City Magazine* (December 1988).

Stogdill, R. M. *Handbook of Leadership.* New York: Free Press, 1974.

Taylor, Penelope. "Intrapreneurial Climate Factors in Innovative School Districts." Ed.D. diss., University of La Verne, 1980.

Toffler, Alvin. *The Third Wave.* New York: Morrow, 1980.

Vroom, Victor Harold. *Work and Motivation.* New York: John Wiley, 1964.

Yukl, Gary. *Leadership in Organizations.* Englewood Cliffs, NJ: Prentice Hall, 1981.

Index

About the Authors

Thomas R. Harvey is a professor of Organizational Leadership in the doctoral program at the University of La Verne in La Verne, California, a suburb of Los Angeles. He has been the dean of organizational management and chairman of the Department of Educational Management for fourteen years. He received his B.A. from Princeton University and his Ph.D. from Syracuse University. He has consulted with over 400 businesses, schools, and public institutions, and has been a city councilman for twenty years. He is the author of *Strategies for Significant Survival, Checklist for Change* (ScarecrowEducation, 1995) and coauthor of *The Practical Decision Maker* (ScarecrowEducation, 1997).

Dr. Harvey is an avid family man who enjoys playing golf with his two sons, Scott and Andy, and bringing laughter to his grandchildren, Loryn and Kalyn. He and Bonita Drolet are partners in Management by Design, a consulting firm that emphasizes conflict management, strategic planning, change strategies, and team building.

Bonita M. Drolet is an assistant superintendent of educational services for the Encinitas Union School District in San Diego County, California. Previously, she was an elementary principal in the Placentia–Yorba Linda Unified School District in Orange County, California. She honed her passion for improving education while serving as a principal in Ontario, California, and Charter Oak, California, before moving to Bryant Ranch School. At Bryant Ranch, a National Blue Ribbon School, she was able to actualize the creation and implementation of the ideas and strategies found in *Building Teams, Building People*.

She received her bachelor's and master's degrees from California State University, Los Angeles, and earned a doctorate of educational management at the University of La Verne.

Dr. Drolet has consulted with numerous organizations including schools, businesses, and public organizations. She has chaired numerous professional organizations throughout her career as an educational leader. She and Thomas Harvey are partners in Management by Design and in marriage. She enjoys traveling both for work and pleasure, which allows time for another passion—reading. She spends her free time with her sons and the fabulous women in their lives, Robyn, Stacy, Loryn, Kalyn, and Emma.